MW00440039

Book 2, The Pet Bereavement Series

My Dog Has Died: What Do I Do?

Making Decisions and Healing the Trauma of Pet Loss

Wendy Van de Poll, MS, CEOL

ISBN: 978-0-9973756-1-9

DISCLAIMER

If you are ever feeling like you can no longer function with your life, become suicidal, and any of the normal grief feelings have become extreme for you, then that is considered unhealthy grief. This is the time to call your hospital, medical practitioner, psychologist, or other health care provider that is trained to help you. Do not isolate yourself if you are experiencing unhealthy grief. Get the professional help that you require.

THANK YOU!

Thank you for purchasing *My Dog Has Died: What Do I Do?* To show my appreciation, I'm offering this special gift to support your journey because I am compassionately dedicated to helping you...my valued reader.

Healing Dog Loss Meditation.mp3 will help calm the chaos and anxiety that you may be experiencing.

To Download Your **FREE GIFT**

Healing Dog Loss Meditation.mp3

Please Go To:
www.centerforpetlossgrief.com/book-2-gift-sign-page

This book is dedicated to the little rescue puppy that flew by jet from Texas to NH. Addie you knew that you were coming home before I did. You are my light and you single handedly rescued my heart when it was split wide open.

Contents

Introduction

You just arrived home and walked through the door. For a second you realize that something is very different. Your house is quiet, there is a feeling of emptiness, and for some reason it feels cold. These feelings are taking on a life of their own, and suddenly reality hits you!

It only takes seconds for this to happen, before you realize that your dog is not bounding through the house to greet you. Your dog is no longer enveloping you with unconditional love, kisses, and endless joy.

You ask yourself, "What am I going to do?"

The answer to this question—and the good news—is what I'm sharing in this book. I'm offering tools to support you through your grief and guide you on how to deal with all the changes that you are going to experience immediately after the death of your dog as well as support on how to prepare for the future. In this book, I supply you with options for ways to rescue yourself from the potentially overwhelming pet loss emotions when your dog is no longer physically with you. I will support you right away.

This book is for you if your dog has died and you are experiencing grief, having difficulty making important decisions, and you want to do something special to not forget the life you shared with your dog.

Plus, if you want to never lose the connection that you had with your dog and are looking for ways to have them spiritually in your life, you will find solutions in this book.

My Dog Has Died: What Do I Do? Making Decisions and Healing the Trauma of Pet Loss has been written to give you options and tools for navigating your personal journey through this raw and challenging time, a time filled with so many emotions and unexpected experiences. It is here as a handbook to keep with you as a constant guide to offer support in this particular phase of losing your dog.

My Dog Has Died: What Do I Do? will help you gain a deeper spiritual understanding of why your dog was in your life and to show you that even though they are not physically with you, your special and unique spiritual relationship with them will continue to grow. You will learn ways to talk to your dog, so you can experience their presence never completely leaving you.

Something special I'm offering in this book that I've not found in other pet grief books is contemplation questions, plus a free, downloadable Healing Dog Loss Meditation mp3 to help you calm the chaos and anxiety that you may be experiencing. At the end of each chapter, you will find three *Contemplation Questions*, designed to help you proceed even more profoundly and personally in your journey. When you become a dynamic participant in managing your grief, the changes and growth that you experience become very personal.

You see—I know these feelings of grief very well as I have been there with my own dogs. With each one, I learned something very beautiful and joyful in my life. After Marley's death, when I rescued my own grief by adopting Addie, I began to understand a new chapter in my life. In many ways, Addie added on to what I learned from Marley, my beloved dog who is featured in *Book 1: My Dog Is Dying: What Do I Do? Emotions, Decisions, and Options for Healing.*

Along with my personal experiences, plus being a certified end-of-life and pet loss grief coach (CEOL), a tested animal medium and communicator, as well as a licensed massage therapist for humans, horses, and hounds, I have helped countless people around the world to be able to embrace their forever relationships that they had with their dogs even after their beloved dogs died.

People who feel alone, lost, and despair after their dogs died have found comfort, calmness, and sanctity from the continued reinforcement of support with this book. They discover and understand that the spiritual relationship that we all have with our dogs continues even after they are no longer physically with us.

Anne, whose dog Ruby died of liver cancer, explained, "The best thing about this book is that it can immediately calm your fear and despair by showing you how even though your dog has died, they are not gone forever. There is an immeasurable part of their soul that is deeply connected to you. I learned that my fear was normal yet important to express through mourning so that my spiritual connection with Ruby would grow within me through this journey."

I promise you that when you follow the tips, explore the *Contemplation Questions*, and download your free gift you will not feel as lost, alone, or even panicked about the loss of your dog.

Instead, you will know how to deal with your family, friends, and coworkers when their eyes glaze over when you express your grief and they tell you to move on. You will learn how to make some really tough decisions, like how to care for your dog's body. Plus, you will learn new and healthy ways to mourn and what to expect with your "new normal."

Finally, if you believe in the spiritual nature of things and that the existence of energy is infinite, you will explore universal knowledge about how your dog is still connected to you in the spirit form. This book will teach you how to access your dog's energy, so you can continue learning about what your dog has to tell you.

Your grieving process after the death of your dog is delicate, unique, and extremely important. Because your beloved companion died, this book will support you through the stages of grief, the mourning period, and beyond. It can be an extremely difficult time—your life suddenly is not normal anymore because you lost your closest companion. It can take time to find a new normal.

As you read this book, be prepared for the things that you will experience and learn. Know that you are no longer alone in your journey and you can actively look at death in a different way.

When you actively take death by the hand and engage with your emotions, decisions, and healing from your trauma of grief, you will be able to make changes in your life. You will be able to hear your body, mind, and soul, and begin to celebrate the beauty of your dog and how much they influenced the person you are today. Be the person who looks at the pet loss grief journey as an opportunity to not fear death and as a journey to learn, love, and heal.

This book that you are about to read will help you to choose ways to experience your pet loss with compassion, forgiveness, respect, and love for yourself and your dog. It is a rough and hard-hitting time for your heart. If you perceive your loss as a finality, try to open your heart and realize that your dog is part of you forever.

Remember, your dog loves you and has a very special place in your soul. Knowing and embracing this love will help heal your trauma so that you will never feel alone again.

LIFE WITHOUT YOUR DOG BEGINS: SECTION ONE

"Should you shield the valleys from the windstorms, you would never see the beauty of their canyons."

—Elisabeth Kubler-Ross

1. Detecting Your Feelings of Grief

You don't need anyone telling you that the life you shared with your dog was the best! Your life was filled with adventures, events, soft moments, and unconditional love. The memories that you cherish are what will keep you sane and connected to your dog forever.

Yet, right now everything is different and new for you. Your dog is no longer physically with you, and you are noticing some very uncomfortable feelings that you are unsure of. Your emotions may be creating chaos in your life—you may be feeling extreme anxiety or even depression. You may be unsure of what to do next.

Many of my clients ask me, "Does my sadness over the loss of my dog ever go away?" I would like to answer yes, but to be perfectly honest with you, the answer is no. However, by understanding what grief is and by employing the great tools and support that I offer you in this book, you are going to find that you are not alone. You will be able to navigate this tough journey with respect, forgiveness, and love—for both your dog and you.

If you read my first book in this series, *My Dog Is Dying: What Do I Do? Emotions, Decisions, and Options for Healing*, you read a lot about the characteristics of normal grief. Although there are many similarities with experiencing grief while your dog is alive, your grief will change after they are no longer in your life.

As you continue your journey of grief or are just starting out with pet loss, I encourage you to consider this book as a new best friend that will guide you and walk the journey of pet loss grief with you.

I will help you understand what normal grief is and how you can begin to cope with it in this chapter.

Normal and Healthy Grief

If you are you feeling hopeless right now because you don't know whom to talk to, how to get help, or whom to get help from—you are experiencing normal grief. This chapter will help you understand and support this uncomfortable but normal feeling.

If your blood is starting to boil because you are so angry that your best friend died or if you are feeling guilty, depressed, numb, or even shock—you are experiencing normal pet grief, and the tools in this book will help you process those feelings so that you will be able to celebrate the life you had with your dog.

Once you understand what normal grief is and what the expectations are for you, your journey will become different—and more manageable.

Case Study — Carmon and Jetson

When Carmon came home after she had to euthanize her twelve-year-old Border collie named Jetson, she was beyond devastated. When she came to me, it had been two weeks since Jetson died, and she hadn't slept, eaten, or talked to anyone. She even took sick days from work, so she could be alone.

In our first conversation, Carmon was so distraught that she wasn't even able to form complete sentences when explaining the situation to me. She cried hysterically, had bouts of rage mixed with sadness, and, at times, just couldn't articulate what she was feeling.

Now here is the thing—Carmon was having a healthy reaction to her loss. No, Carmon's grief was not easy or comfortable, but it was healthy.

I know that sounds weird, but this is how it works: the fact that Carmon could outwardly express herself to someone, who was non-judgmental and could listen to what she had to say without adding advice or suggestions, is what helped Carmon understand and cope with her grief, which, in turn, made her grief experience less fear-and anxiety-ridden.

Just to clarify further, even though Carmon's grief was normal, that didn't mean it was easy or short-lived. Carmon was feeling weird about her feelings and was not comfortable with what was going on in her mind, in her body, and with her spiritual beliefs. And this is part of the normal, but unpleasant, grief experience.

Carmon also suffered from a huge amount of guilt after Jetson died. She felt guilty about not doing more for Jetson when he was alive, like the times that he wanted to go outside and Carmon ignored his requests. Again, feeling such guilt is heart-wrenching but also—normal.

During our conversation, I encouraged Carmon to talk about everything that she was feeling and going through—all the feelings that were driving her crazy and how she was going to begin to share this news with others.

The result—Carmon began to make sense of the myriad of feelings and physical sensations she was experiencing. She began to understand that what she was going through was very difficult but also—normal.

Plus, she learned that her original expectation—that she could avoid feeling grief—was not realistic. When this expectation changed and she realized that grief was healthy, she felt much better.

Over the course of our working together in my Rescue Joy from Pet Loss Grief program, Carmon learned that her experiences of pet grief were difficult and uncomfortable but, at the same time, normal, healthy, and special.

By understanding her feelings and accepting those crazy thoughts, sensations, and spiritual upheavals, she began to walk the journey of losing the physical Jetson with respect for herself. This, in turn, gave her the direction and focus she needed to be present for the possibilities of a continued relationship with Jetson on a spiritual level.

When our conversation for that day ended, Carmon wasn't free from feeling grief. Yet, she had more strength and grounding to move forward to contemplate her next moment in this special journey.

Element 1 — Normal and Necessary

What Carmon's story demonstrates is that the first thing about pet grief after your dog has died is to know that what you are feeling and thinking, though uncomfortable and difficult, is also normal and healthy. Grief is necessary, so it is critical that you let your feelings happen.

If you stuff grief down, so many detrimental things can happen to your health and well-being. Stuffing grief down will affect how you live—in a negative way—from the day your dog dies, to how you will mourn, and to how you begin to move forward.

In fact, if you stuff your feelings down, your normal grief feelings can become unhealthy and result in unhealthy actions. We will talk about unhealthy grief later in this chapter.

Normal Grief Feelings — A List

Here are some normal feelings of pet grief that you may experience now or later in your journey.

- *Physical* ~ crying, sobbing, wailing, numbness, dry mouth, nausea, tightness in the chest, restlessness, fatigue, sleep disturbance, appetite disturbance, dizziness, fainting, or shortness of breath

- *Intellectual* ~ sense of unreality, inability to concentrate, feeling preoccupied with the loss, hallucinations concerning the loss, a sense that time is passing very slowly, or a desire to rationalize feelings about the loss

- *Emotional* ~ anger, depression, guilt, anxiety, relief, irritability, desire to blame others for the loss, self-doubt, lowered self-esteem, feeling overwhelmed, or feeling out of control, hopeless, or helpless

- *Social* ~ feelings of isolation or alienation, feeling rejected by others, or a reluctance to ask for help

- *Spiritual* ~ feeling angry at your deity after your dog died and blaming them for the loss or even bargaining to try and get your dog back.

A Life of Its Own

As you can see, normal grief is varied and expansive. The thing about grief is that it has a life of its own. What this means is that you can be going through a quiet period of your journey when you are feeling relatively good. Then something happens, and it triggers intense, and perhaps unexpected, feelings of pet grief.

I am here to tell you to let this happen. Let yourself feel what you are going through. Let those feelings rage. Let your tears flow. It's healthy and necessary.

Abnormal Grief Feelings

Yet, if you are ever feeling like you can no longer function with your life or if you become suicidal and any of the normal grief feelings become extreme, then that is considered unhealthy grief. This is the time to call your hospital, medical practitioner, psychologist, or a health care provider that is trained to help you. Do not isolate yourself if you are experiencing unhealthy grief. Get the professional help that you require.

Element 2 — Reach Out

In addition to recognizing your normal grief feelings, a second essential component for navigating your pet grief journey is to reach out to someone else, as Carmon did. Look for someone who will listen to every word of your conversation with respect and compassion, and share your grief experience with this person. In doing this, you will feel better about what you are going through, you will feel supported, and you will come to better understand your own grief.

Element 3 — Spend Time with Your Memories

Spend time with your memories. Look at photos, write down special moments, and reflect on the intense love that you shared with your furry friend. By doing this exercise, you can calm your raging emotions and begin to develop a different kind of relationship with your dog, one which we will talk about more in chapters 12, 13, and 15.

Element 4 — Know Your Grief Feelings

Also, it is important to be familiar with your unique grief feelings. Everyone grieves differently, so get to know your own grief. Your feelings are going to be with you every single day, and when I help my clients understand their grief, it becomes less of a burden or something to fear. You are going to be spending a lot of time with your feelings over the next few days, months, and even years, so it is important that you come to know them and you don't fear them.

Spend some time responding to the three *Contemplation Questions* at the end of this chapter. These questions will help guide you to recognize your own unique feelings of normal pet grief that you are experiencing.

Chapter Wrap-Up

Losing your dog is extremely difficult. Your dog was your constant companion. You both loved each other unconditionally.

The first twenty-four hours is one of the most difficult transitions to experience.

Try to understand your unique feelings of grief and spend time just being in the moment by breathing and preparing yourself for the journey to come. Revisit the four elements I've given you in this chapter and begin to internalize and act upon them. Respond to the chapter's *Contemplation Questions* to help you manage your normal, but uncomfortable, feelings of grief.

In chapter 2, I am going to teach you the seven stages of grief that you may or may not experience in full due to the death of your dog. With each of these stages, I am going to give you examples of what you can expect from yourself as well as from other people.

Chapter 1 Contemplation Questions

What feelings of grief do you have now?

How are you dealing with these feelings? Can you make a list of your feelings, arranging them with the most intense feelings first down to the least charged emotions?

If you have any abnormal feelings of grief, write down your health care practitioner's contact information and have it readily available.

2. Riding Your Stages of Grief and Loss

As I shared in the first chapter, your grief has a life of its own. If you are feeling sad, angry, or like your heart has been ripped open—please understand that this is absolutely okay.

We all experience these feelings in different ways and at different times. By remembering that your grief is unique and special to the relationship that you had with your dog, you can be ready for the stages that you will be experiencing with less confusion or difficulty.

Keep in mind there is more to your journey of coping than the fact that your dog is no longer physically in your life.

Pet loss grief actually has seven identifiable stages. By understanding these seven stages of grief, your disorder of emotions and possible shock about what you are now faced with can change, so you can hopefully feel less stress as you move through these stages.

Learning which stage of pet loss grief you are experiencing is extremely helpful to your coping and healing journey. You can gain compassion and respect for your own process, both of which are vital to finding joy after suffering so much intense grief from your loss.

Living without your dog is ridiculously difficult. The shock, horror, and unrelenting pain can easily take you away from taking care of yourself. By exploring the stages of grief, you can begin to learn self-compassion and gain a needed understanding of your journey.

No matter what you are experiencing after the death of your dog, one of the most important things to remember is to cherish the life you had with them. The memories you have are beautiful, and the stages of grief that you are experiencing will only have a positive effect on your continued relationship with your dog.

The grief that you are feeling right now is perfect, so please be kind to yourself and not expect anything more or anything less. It is there, and it's not going to go away. Yet, it will change as time progresses.

The Seven Stages of Grief

It is extremely helpful to know not only what normal grief is but also what the normal stages of grief are.

Dr. Elisabeth Kubler-Ross was a pioneer in the hospice movement. While she wasn't a pet grief person, what she discovered can be applied to the journey of pet grief.

In 1969, in her book *On Death and Dying*, Dr. Kubler-Ross made the five steps of grief and/or death well known. The following five steps cover the stages of grieving for the death of a loved one.

1. Denial
2. Anger
3. Bargaining
4. Depression
5. Acceptance

These five stages became very popular and are recognized widely, mostly during the dying process. However, people working in this field began to expand on her various philosophies and standards. Currently, there are seven stages of grief.

These are the seven stages of grief that I use in my practice when helping people like you explore their pet grief and loss stages. These stages will guide you to a deeper understanding of what you are experiencing with your feelings.

1. Shock and Denial

2. Pain and Guilt

3. Anger and Bargaining

4. Depression, Reflection, and Loneliness

5. Adjustment to Life

6. Your New Normal

7. Acceptance and Hope

Over and over my clients tell me that this information is valuable and helps prepare them every day to live more fully and for the future.

Keep in mind that since your journey is yours, you may not experience all of these stages as your daily pet loss progresses. Yet you may. Whatever you experience is normal, so be compassionate with yourself for what you are going through. Never compare your experience to someone else's.

Case Study — Cissy, Crystal, and the Seven Stages

Cissy, a client of mine, experienced all seven stages of grief. She and I started working together eight months after Crystal died. When Cissy recalled her feelings and actions through our conversations, she felt much better and more in control of what she had experienced and was currently experiencing.

Even still, Cissy was confused and worried because she continued to break down in tears whenever she saw a dog that looked like Crystal. Her mother was telling her that eight months was too long to still be crying and that she should be over it by now (the length of the grieving period is something we'll address in chapter 5).

Stage One: Shock and Denial

As we worked together, Cissy began to understand why she felt the unshakable feelings of trauma and not believing that Crystal had died. Cissy recalled that during the first 24 hours of being alone without Crystal, she felt totally in shock and quite dizzy. She remembered literally opening the door to check on Crystal to see if she was sleeping on the porch.

Cissy was traumatized, in shock, and in denial that Crystal wasn't with her any longer. She remembered thinking, "This is not happening to me. It is a mistake. Crystal didn't die. She is just outside chewing her bone on the porch."

Stage Two: Pain and Guilt

Cissy was feeling intense angst and sadness, so much so that her body actually hurt. She was not sure how she really felt at this time, eight months after Crystal's death. I assured her that her feelings were common and in accordance with the second stage of grief.

When this information started to settle in and become more accepted, Cissy's guilt took off like an uncontrolled fire. She went through it all. She felt as if she should have done something differently when Crystal was alive—different food, different treats, a different veterinarian. She even felt like she caused Crystal's death.

Stage Three: Anger and Bargaining

When Cissy got angry, she was unrelenting in blaming herself and her spiritual beliefs. She told me that within the first 24 hours of Crystal's death, she'd begun to bargain and ask her higher power to give her a sign on how she could bring Crystal back to life.

She was so irritated that this was an impossible thing to do. She wanted Crystal back right away. She told me that she really hated herself in the beginning because she believed she had caused Crystal's death. She felt the full responsibility, and her anger was colossal.

She was so distraught that one day she went into her kitchen, took a bunch of old dishes, and started to throw them. She told her higher powers that if they would bring Crystal back, she would make sure that Crystal would always be the center of her attention.

Stage Four: Depression, Reflection, and Loneliness

When Cissy and I started to work together, she was experiencing the fourth stage. She was beginning to understand that anger and bargaining were part of the journey once we'd talked about what she was experiencing.

Her days when she called me were filled with intense crying, numbness, and overwhelming feelings of depression. She told me, "I have no one in my family that understands how important Crystal was to me." Every day she felt as though she were totally alone and isolated within her grief.

As we continued to work together, Cissy began to understand that her feelings of depression and loneliness were part of the grief process. Soon she was able to reflect on the awesome life that she'd had with Crystal.

She even shared with me, "I am so glad I can give myself permission every day to not be afraid of my sadness and loneliness. Once I understood this part of me, I could again experience the loving feelings that I shared with Crystal."

Stage Five: Adjustment to Life

It was very difficult for Cissy to transition out of the previous stage and to stage five. She really didn't want to move on with life without Crystal. She felt that if she allowed herself to feel happy or even get another dog (more on this point in chapter 10), she would be disrespecting Crystal.

She confided one day, "Geez, Wendy, I have felt shock, denial, pain, guilt, anger, depression, and loneliness. I have even been crazy angry at my higher power! I want to move on, but I don't want to disrespect my bond with Crystal. How do I do that?"

This was a great place for Cissy in her grief journey and a question that most of my clients ask. Throughout this book, we will be talking about adjusting to a new life in more detail. Yet for now, keep in mind that this period is about integrating these changes into your daily life to help you rescue your joy and not forget or disrespect your dog.

I have recorded a Healing Dog Loss Meditation to help you calm the chaos and anxiety that you may be experiencing. You can download your free mp3 at the beginning of this book. This meditation will help you adjust to your new life too.

Stage Six: Your New Normal

As time moved on, Cissy began to adjust to the changes and instead of worrying about what other people thought of her grief, she began to look for another dog. She adjusted to the myriad changes in her new life and recognized that her heart was ready to open to another dog. She knew that by getting another dog she wasn't being disrespectful to Crystal and that Crystal still held a very special place in her soul.

She even discovered a support group of individuals in the same situation as hers. Every week Cissy and her group got together and shared stories, heartache, and joy.

Stage Seven: Acceptance and Hope

When Cissy began to experience the last stage of pet grief, she was ready to move forward with an entirely different attitude. She accepted the fact that Crystal had died.

Cissy found her new normal and had a plan of action on how she was going to share her life with her new dog—the food, the doctors, the new activities. Now she could live every day with joy, hope, and a desire to do the best she could with her new dog.

This was the stage when she became more aware and accepted her grief stages. She was confident that she could provide everything that her new dog needed. It was easier to make decisions through whatever stage of grief she was experiencing.

Did Cissy forget Crystal at this stage? No, she did not! She was able to recognize that death is something that we cannot avoid.

Chapter Wrap-Up

These stages are references to guide you on how you can process your particular pet loss grief. Cissy experienced all the stages. By no means do you need to experience them all as Cissy did or even move through the stages in the exact order.

Use the three *Contemplation Questions* at the end of this chapter to help guide you through your unique stages of grief.

Again, please remember that you are not alone in your grief journey. There are others that are experiencing the same thing as you.

In the next chapter, I am going to teach you about the myths that surround pet grief and how these myths can hold you back from healing your grief. I am also going to show you how you can turn these myths around so that they can help you with your journey.

Chapter 2 Contemplation Questions

What are the stages of grief that you have experienced? Are you experiencing them in the presented sequence?

What have you learned about your unique journey through each of these stages? How is it helping you to know what stages you are experiencing?

Wendy helps her clients know and understand the seven stages of pet grief early in their journeys. Her clients find that by knowing this valuable information early on, rather than later, they are better prepared for the future. In what ways do you predict that knowing this information now will help you prepare for the future?

3. Confronting the Common Myths

Now that you have an understanding of what constitutes normal grief (chapter 1) and have explored the seven stages of grief (chapter 2), we are going to visit the multitude of myths that come along with pet grief after your dog dies.

It is important to consider these myths on your healing journey. We have many pre-conceived ideas as to what death is about and how we "should" react to it or dread it. No matter where you are with your beliefs, it is important to approach these myths with an openness and willingness to heal.

To introduce the myths, let's explore the experience of Roberta, a client whom I supported in her grief journey after the loss of her beloved Chester Bell.

Myth Confrontation: Roberta and Chester Bell

My client Roberta, on our fourth call, was incensed about a situation that happened at her book group when one of her group members told her, "Chester Bell was old. He had a good life, and you can always get another dog. They are easy to come by."

Initially in sharing this story, Roberta was screaming it out, but then she started to sob, and next she was laughing uncontrollably. Roberta started to judge herself that she was having such a roller coaster of wild feelings. She was horrified that she had been laughing, which made her start crying again. She told me that she believed it was not right of her to be laughing during this time. Chester Bell had died, so the only feeling she should have was sadness!

My response—"Roberta, that's just a grief myth. Don't you believe it. You are going to live out a variety of emotions, and laughter is just one that you are going to feel on your grief journey."

With my guidance, Roberta permitted herself to have a range of feelings, including laughter, and she strove to understand how unhealthy it was to disrespect her emotions. She allowed the laughter and the tears to come. In doing so, she felt relief. She was able to breathe and understand that laughing was another way to express her grief. She felt as if a heavy weight had been lifted from her heart.

In debunking the "no joy during grieving" myth, Roberta finished her session feeling a lot stronger on her journey. She had renewed confidence that she could heal her pain with more clarity and understanding.

Myths about grieving, like the one Roberta voiced, have been around for a long time, and they can either really help you with your grief or be a hindrance to your healing process. The key to making these myths help you is to be aware of them, know how you feel about them, and then debunk them.

The Myths

1. *It is selfish and extravagant to mourn and grieve the death of a dog when our world has so much human suffering.*

Debunking—You are a dog lover, and you understand how important your dog was to you. The grief surrounding the fact that your dog died is significant and important to you.

People are capable of simultaneously grieving both animals and humans. One doesn't have to detract from the other. By grieving and mourning your dog, you are showing tremendous compassion for the world at large. That is a wonderful trait to have. Realizing that your heart is capable of such love will give you a tremendous amount of strength to heal—and to love again, both animals and people.

2. *I must follow the seven stages of grief in their exact order so that I can truly heal my pain.*

Debunking—Grief is not about following a prescribed list. Grief is tenacious and can really dig into your heart, which can affect your daily routine and then render you hopeless.

The last thing that you need to be worried about is following the seven stages of grief in a precise order. Although the stages of grief are extremely valuable, the order in which you experience them is up to you. Let the stages unfold naturally.

3. *There is a right and wrong way to grieve.*

Debunking—As with following the seven stages of grief in chronological order, the same is true about your unique grief experience—meaning there is not a single correct experience.

Your relationship with your dog is special. No two people grieve the same way. While one person may feel sadness, another person may feel anger about their dog dying. Your grief journey is yours and very unique—stick with that!

Grieving is very personal and individual to your experiences with your dog. It depends on your personality, the personality of your dog, the nature of their illness (if they had one) or death, and your coping style.

4. *The best thing to do is to grieve and mourn alone, especially because it is just a dog.*

Debunking—We have been taught that in order to be strong and independent we should not share our grief. It would burden others, and it is inappropriate to let other people know how we are feeling.

That simply isn't true. In fact, it is important to reach out to others who will honestly support you and not judge your process. You will want to protect yourself from being judged for loving, grieving, and mourning the death of your dog, so it is important that you select carefully the people whom you reach out to. Your experience of loss and grief is a tender time to be fully cherished by you and in the way you decide.

Take your time choosing whom you can turn to for support because some people don't understand or take pet loss seriously. Find a support group, pet loss coach, and/or friend that will allow you to talk about your grief without making you feel crazy or weird. We address this more in chapter 6.

Also remember, if there ever comes a time when you can no longer function in life, please see the appropriate health care provider.

5. *I have to be "strong" in my grief.*

Debunking—In general our society teaches that grief feelings can be a sign of weakness, especially in regards to animals.

Feeling sad, frightened, lonely, or depressed are all normal reactions. Crying doesn't mean that you are weak. In fact, it takes strength to accept and engage with these difficult emotions and to cry.

Let yourself feel those emotions, physical sensations, and spiritual challenges that you are going through. There is a reason you are having these feelings. Plus, there is no reason why you need to feel that you have to "protect" your family or friends by being (supposedly) strong.

Showing your feelings will help you and may even help them. By showing your feelings, you are also debunking the first myth of being selfish. When you show your feelings, you are saying, "I have compassion for living beings." And that, my friend, is extremely beautiful!

6. *Grief will go away someday.*

Debunking—Never! And that is okay. Our grief changes as each day goes by. You will never forget your dog, yet your feelings of grief will change, and there will be a time when you will feel joy again.

Never feel like you have to rush through your grief journey. It takes time. Patience and not judging yourself come in handy when you are experiencing the stages of grief.

Your goal for healing your pet loss is not to "get over it." We never stop feeling grief for losing a pet. But we learn to move forward in life again with fond memories.

7. *No one gets my pet grief, and I am alone in what I am experiencing.*

Debunking—You are never alone with the grief that you are going through. It may feel like that at times because some people don't know what it feels like to lose the companionship of their dogs. They just don't understand what you are going through.

People (even dog lovers) will say unsupportive things, like "There are so many dogs that need homes. See this as an opportunity!" or "At least it wasn't a child."

Even still, there are many, many people who do know the grief you are experiencing. It just may take some time to find the right people to support you in a healthy way. There are supportive friends, end-of-life and grief coaches, and pet loss support groups to walk the journey with you. We will talk about this more in chapter 6.

Remember—you are not alone with your pet loss grief.

8. *Pet loss grief will go away.*

Debunking—Many of my clients call me when they have just gotten the news that their dogs died. Some even call me years later. They feel a tremendous amount of grief and just want it to go away.

It takes work to heal pet loss grief. Feel comfortable and take taking your time. Be an active participant so that you can experience the stages of grief.

Your dog was really special to you. It is really important to let your emotions happen and to experience them. If you feel like they will go away on their own, you are only stuffing them in. The grief will still change, but it may take longer, and you may not learn how powerful grief lessons can be.

And as many of my clients say, "Grief has a great talent of surprising you when you least expect it." So it is better to actively acknowledge, process, and experience it than to stuff it down only for it to pop up at surprising times and in unwelcoming forms.

9. *Once I do all the grief work, it will go away.*

Debunking—Once you do all the work in your grieving process, remember that grief can come up again. It is not uncommon to have deep feelings of grief appear again, even years later. It is normal for this to happen.

Grief never goes away, and that is okay. Many of my clients report that when their grief shows up after a few months or years, they are happy about it because it gives them a chance to say, "I love you," to their dogs again.

For now, if you just lost your dog or are just beginning to work on your grief, tuck this thought in a special place, so you know what to expect later.

10. *Having a feeling of joy at moments in my life after my dog has died is not good.*

Debunking—Here is the thing—your companion has died. Your dog was maybe very sick or elderly, or suffered a traumatic death.

The last thing that you probably think you are allowed to feel is joyful or happy. In fact, you probably are feeling many emotions from this news. All your emotions are valid and okay to feel.

It is okay to experience moments of joy, even when you are grieving about your dog's death. It is healthy and doesn't mean you are forgetting your dog's situation or disrespecting your dog.

Joy and laughter are normal responses. This is your body giving you a breather from the stress, pain, anxiety, etc. It is a survival mechanism that you do not need to fear. Joy is first aid for the soul.

11. *It is horrible to feel happy or relieved that my dog died.*

Debunking—If you had a dog that was suffering, there may be a little place in your mind that felt relief once they died.

If this is so, when the time has come and your dog has reached the end of their life, you may feel relieved and even slightly glad. This is a very common feeling for my clients that suffered the pain and angst of losing their dogs to terminal illnesses.

When your dog is in pain and suffering every day, it can take a lot out of you, emotionally, physically, and spiritually. It breaks your heart and can leave you feeling hopeless and helpless. At your dog's death, feeling slightly glad and even relieved are also very normal feelings of grief. Keep in mind that these are not due to selfishness, but simply feelings that your dog is no longer suffering in the physical world.

The Other Side of the Myths: Grace and Compassion

These myths are very common, and many people think they are true. These myths, in conjunction with the inappropriate comments that people make (more on these in chapter 4), can easily trigger your grief. If you are not aware of the myths, you may become confused as to why suddenly you are feeling sad or very angry.

Even though they may be well-meaning friends, family, or coworkers, when one of them offers you a myth as a so-called "word of wisdom," it can pack a powerful punch to trigger your pet loss grief. However, once you become aware of these myths and why they are not true, you will be able to react to them with grace and compassion for yourself and your beloved companion.

Here is the thing about believing these myths and letting them affect you—I have seen in my practice that when folks believe and live by these myths, they get stuck in their grief and have a difficult time gaining personal peace.

When they learn to take these myths, debunk them, and replace them with positive thoughts and actions, they are able to spend more time loving their dogs that have died, rather than being stressed-out with unknown anxiety or other feelings of grief that they may be experiencing.

Please revisit these myths and the debunking of them. They will help you be prepared for the multitude of thoughts and feelings that you will have and the comments people will make.

Use the chapter's three *Contemplation Questions* to help you to identify and then debunk any myths that you may encounter in your journey.

Chapter Wrap-Up

Myths about pet loss grief can be roadblocks to moving forward with meaning and purpose in regard to the bond you have with your pet.

The way to remove the roadblocks and make the myths work for you is to be aware of them, debunk them, and then replace them with something positive.

To repeat, always remember—you are not alone in your grief journey. There are others that are experiencing the same thing as you. Find those people and spend time with them.

In chapter 4, I am going to help you prepare for the insensitive things that people will say to you and how these statements can trigger your grief unexpectedly. I am also going to show you how to be aware of these statements before they happen, so you can prepare yourself and won't be totally thrown if you encounter them.

Chapter 3 Contemplation Questions

Since your dog is no longer physically with you, have you experienced any myths given in this chapter? If so, reflect on that experience.

Now that you have encountered several of the common myths surrounding pet loss grief, add other myths that you may be experiencing. Can you debunk them and pull something positive out of them?

Notice which myths you relate to. Write them down and then rewrite them in a positive way. Post them in a prominent place so that frequently you can be reminded what is really true.

4. Understanding Why They Said That

When a family member, coworker, stranger you meet at the gym, or even your best friend tries to reassure you by commenting, "My goodness, you are still grieving? . . . Isn't it time to move on?" you may immediately feel hurt and then ask yourself, "What did I just hear?"

You may find that you start to feel the hair on your arms stand on end. Physically, you may feel off-center. Quite abruptly, you may feel extremely sad. Likely your well-being changes. You start to feel uncomfortable, yet you don't know what to do. Should you just smile and say, "Thank you," or should you just politely turn away and go about your business?

The first thing to come to terms with is that people are going to say hurtful things like this to you. People want to be helpful, so they'll say these things that they think are helpful and well-meaning. However, in reality their words about your beloved companion's death are totally off the mark and very unsupportive so much so that they can trigger an unexpected feeling or reaction. I will warn you, most of the time you will feel unprepared for these unsupportive statements.

What is happening when people say these unintentionally unsupportive things is that they are inadvertently fueling and activating your grief. You become sad, depressed, angry, or confused, and you are not sure why, all of a sudden, you are feeling this way. You likely become confused as to how to handle these people and even wonder if you should continue being friends.

Let me repeat—it is normal for people to say unsupportive, yet what they think are well-meaning, things to someone who has lost a dog. And it is also customary for you to have the uncomfortable and confusing reactions that you are having.

Now here is the thing—as a society we have gotten very distant from the dying process. We view it as something to be afraid of, and we may even want to avoid it. As people, the more we accept death and allow our grief to happen in a safe environment, then the healthier this process will be.

Remember—your confused and heightened reaction to the person's statement is common, and it is important to not believe or internalize what they have said.

I am going to teach you in this chapter how you can use what you've learned about grief itself (from chapter 1) and the stages of grief (from chapter 2), so you can handle the situation with compassion, respect, and grace.

Case Study — Ellissa and Lester

Ellissa, whose dog Lester died suddenly in a car accident, told me in one of our sessions that after she'd told her best friend about Lester, her friend started to avoid her.

Ellissa was confused and felt very alone. She explained, "My dog just got hit by a car, so I felt helpless and hopeless. I wanted help right away. All I wanted was my best friend, someone to talk to, but she is now avoiding me and has said some really hurtful things."

You can expect this to happen to you. Because, as with Ellissa's experience, people dread death, so some will avoid dealing with it—no matter what. As a society we aren't versed in how to go about supporting each other in a healthy way when someone is experiencing grief of any kind.

When Ellissa became aware of the unsupportive things her best friend and others were saying, she prepared herself on how she was going to react. The beautiful result of this is she found that her support team suddenly grew and she had new friends that truly understood and supported her.

Your Preparation

Right now I want to share how you can be prepared for the hurtful things that people will say to you.

I promise you are going to hear them every day, not from everyone, but you will hear them from people that you thought understood what you are going through—just like what happened with Ellissa.

This is a huge part of your journey when dealing with your dog's death. Be ready, be prepared, and take control of these situations, so you know that what you are feeling is okay and normal.

Here are a few of the many things people typically say that my clients have experienced. (At the end of this chapter, you will have the opportunity to list some of your own.)

Hurtful Things That People Say

1. *It's only a dog . . .* You can get another.

As a dog parent, you know that the relationship that you had with your dog was unique to the both of you. No one else had the relationship as you two did.

When someone says to you, "It's only a dog, and you can get another," this is the time for you to respond, "Thank you," and make your exit. To engage and try to educate this person only takes time and can be extremely exhausting. It is your sole job when experiencing grief to not exert your emotional and physical energies on those that do not understand.

2. *I am so sorry to hear that.*

This one is a big one and the most popular thing to say when we get the news that someone's dog died. The fact is that it is not that person's fault that your dog reached the end of their life.

I know it may be a moot point, but a kinder, more supportive, and compassionate way to respond to this type of news is "I am so sad to hear that your dog died. Would you like me to listen to what you are feeling?" This type of comment will give you a safe place to express your grief rather than feeling like you have to take care of the other person's sadness or have to protect yourself from feeling even more grief.

The way you can react to the "I am sorry" response is NOT to thank them. Because, remember, it is not your job to take care of someone else. Silence, a small smile, followed by a gentle head nod is all that is needed. If they persist, you can politely excuse yourself.

3. *You are still grieving?*

"You are still grieving?" is a very insensitive question to pose to someone that is feeling sad or depressed that their dog died. It suggests that there should be a time limit on the grief process and that you've taken it too far.

Prepare yourself by falling back on what you've learned about grief thus far in the book—grieving doesn't just go away, and it does not have a timetable. Remember, take as much time as is necessary with your grieving.

This question oftentimes helps people know who their real support team is. If you hear this, you can politely respond, "Yes, I am," and then make your exit. You really don't want to waste your time with people that just don't get it.

4. *Let me tell you what I did after my dog died.*

This is another tough one. Although it may seem supportive, it can also be overwhelming and create feelings of guilt. Your dog may have just died or you are six months into your grief journey. You may be trying to figure out where all the pieces of the puzzle go in your new situation. Opening yourself up to a ton of advice at this time could be helpful, but it could also increase your feelings of anxiety, guilt, hopelessness, and being overwhelmed.

You can pick and choose what advice you want to listen to. We will explore this in more detail later in this book by giving you ways to make decisions based on your own terms, beliefs, and experiences.

However, right now, a good way to respond to this fourth comment is, "I appreciate your thoughts of concern, but I really just need to process my feelings at this time."

Please use the three *Contemplation Questions* at the end of this chapter to guide you to become aware of and prepare your reaction to these kinds of statements.

Your Support Team

You are the expert when it comes to your grief journey after your dog is no longer physically in your life. Your grief journey is unique, and no two people deal the same way with losing a dog to a life threatening-illness, age, or traumatic accident.

The important thing to remember is to choose the people that you interact with wisely during this special time. Choose those that truly support you, listen, don't judge you, and only give you advice when you ask them.

That type of support is available to you. You don't need to feel alone and go through this journey without support and compassion.

When you find these people, consider them friends to help you never have to walk the journey of pet loss grief alone again. In chapter 6, we will talk about ways in which you can get support.

Chapter Wrap-Up

This chapter is aimed at helping you become aware of the unsupportive things that people are going to say to you while you are coping with pet loss. This is common—and it is also understandable that their words will trigger grief in you.

The key to responding to such statements with compassion and grace is to prepare yourself and to entrench yourself in the truth about grief (chapter 1) and its seven stages (chapter 2). You will use this chapter's *Contemplation Questions* to help you to become aware of and prepare your reaction to these statements.

Also, you may want to actively find one, two, or more people who will serve as your "support team," listening to you and allowing you to live out your grief as it naturally happens.

In chapter 5, I am going to share with you ways that our society puts high demands on our emotions and how we process them. It is not considered a positive thing when we take time out of our fast-paced lives to mourn our losses. Instead, we are encouraged to get over them fast and not take the appropriate time to heal. You will gain an understanding on how to bust through those demands so that you are able to grieve and pay tribute to your memories.

Chapter 4 Contemplation Questions

Which "Hurtful Things That People Say" comments have you heard? Have you received other comments that triggered your grief? If so, write them down.

How did you respond to the statements that you listed above, and how did you support yourself and/or take control of the situation?

List the names of the people that you are comfortable with and how they are supporting you. Do you seek them out on a daily, weekly, or monthly basis?

5. Expecting What Will Happen After

After your dog dies, many changes are going to happen to you besides your personal grief journey. Your life is going to change and things are going to be different now that your companion is no longer with you.

You are going to be faced with needing to make some important decisions about burial, cremation, or when it is appropriate to get another dog. You are also going to be challenged to be mindful of your own health as you navigate your changed life.

As mentioned already, it is essential and important to take all the time that you need for your grieving and then to know what to expect during this process in order to heal your pet loss.

We live in a society that has high demands on our emotions and how we process them. It is not considered a positive act when we take time out of our fast-paced lives to experience and mourn our losses. Instead, we are encouraged to get over them fast and not take the appropriate time to heal.

Because of societal norms, we often become impatient with our grieving and healing, and have forgotten that quality takes time. When your dog dies and you are experiencing grief, it just cannot be rushed and expected of you to get on with your life.

As you learned in chapters 1 and 2, grief is normal and has a life of its own, and it is perfectly common to feel the way you do. From the myths and unsupportive comments others may make, you also learned that grief is feared by our society.

Since our society is very fast-paced, we are expected to move through our feelings without much notice and get back to being productive right away. We are rushed to return to work and encouraged to stop crying and to get over loss in lightning speed time. There's an entire list of other expectations that can be nearly impossible when facing grief.

Yet, wouldn't it be wonderful if we would slow down and allow our emotions to heal on their own terms?

Case Study — Piper and Dandelion

I had a client named Piper who called me six months after her dog, Dandelion, died. Dandelion died of cancer, and it was a very difficult process for her.

When Piper called me, she was extremely stressed out that she was still feeling her grief—six months after Dandelion's death. She confided, "It is long enough. I don't want to feel this way anymore. My friends and family are telling me to move on and get another dog, and it is driving me crazy that it's taking me so long. Plus, I feel really bad that I feel this way."

During our sessions, I helped Piper discover that her unique journey of pet loss grief could not be rushed. Feeling and expecting to get over it quickly was not a healthy way of dealing with her grief. Her life with Dandelion was so endearing, rich with activities, and awesome that to rush herself was an unfair expectation.

Instead, I encouraged Piper to face her grief and emotions—to engage with them. And if she did the work that it takes to be present in her stages of grief and mourning, her grief experience would become less raw. In my practice, I encourage clients to take the time that they need to heal.

Since there is no timetable for getting over your grief, there are different stages in the grief journey. Some are more difficult than others, and that difficulty is unique to the relationship that you had with your dog. You explored these stages in chapter 2.

However, just like the different stages, keep in mind as you explore the days, weeks, months, and even years after your loss that time will be one of your greatest healers and is on your side a hundred percent. Even though you may feel that you cannot survive another day because the grief is so overwhelming, you can and you will.

The First Days and Weeks After

Here is what you may experience during the first few days and weeks after your dog dies . . .

- My clients often feel numb during the first few days and weeks. There are so many changes during this time, and it takes some getting used to, not having to take care of your buddy. Life becomes a blur.

- It can also be draining and painful. Your grief demands attention, and the newness of your loss starts to settle in.

- The void that you are probably feeling is beyond huge, and there is absolutely nothing that you can do to fill such emptiness. This numbness is part of normal grief that we talked about in chapter 1, yet you might be feeling other emotions as well.

- One of these is denial, which is huge and very common during this time. You may be feeling that it was a bad dream or some mistake or maybe your dog is just outside, enjoying the sunshine, and will be coming in shortly for dinner.

- This denial can even be stronger if their death was sudden or accidental. Many times it lasts longer than it does when you lose a dog to illness or old age.

- Anger and intense frustration are common emotions during this early time period and can easily continue for years.

My client Piper was deeply frustrated and angry with herself that she couldn't cure Dandelion while Dandelion was still alive. She was frustrated that Dandelion was gone and that she hadn't been able to help her live a longer life.

One of the best things that you can do during this time is "nothing." Seriously, you do not need to clean the house, rake the lawn, do errands, or go to the movies with friends if you do not want to. However, if any of these activities will help you feel better, then by all means do them.

It is truly not the time to go deep with trying to process your grief.

It is often very helpful to relax and give yourself permission to feel your loss. It is also a time to be sure that you are eating healthy and doing something that is nurturing for yourself. That may be spending time in nature or getting a massage (more in chapter 6).

Three Months After

It takes about three months for your grief to intensify, and in my experience, the three-month time period is extremely painful and challenging.

Your shock, denial, and disbelief are starting to wear off, and you are beginning to understand the reality of the death of your beloved companion.

It can also be a time when your friends, family, and coworkers have moved on themselves so are encouraging you now to move on too. This can add to the intensity of grief because you may start wondering what is wrong with you.

Having a pet loss grief coach or pet loss support team can be really important for you at this time because they will provide you with the needed support and care by giving you a calm place to express your grief and mourn. They will listen to your story without judgment.

First Anniversary of the Death

I never had a client that forgot the anniversary of the first year of their dog's death. Because it marks such a painful time in the history of the life that you spent together, how could you not feel intense grief?

The pain of your grief will be just as intense as it was when you experienced your initial feelings of loss. Also, be aware that your anticipation of the anniversary date can be as painful, if not worse than, the anniversary itself.

Eleven Years Later— Katharine and Dino

Read what Katharine shares about her feelings eleven years after her dog Dino's death:

> *"It's now eleven years since Dino died. Each year, on the 27th of December, my heart remembers my beloved beagle boy. Each one of our beloved pets has a day marked for remembrance and moments of quiet contemplation and thanks for the joy they brought. Tears no longer flow. Smiles and love bring peace on their days."*

It is important for you to have support and be able to talk through and plan how you want to spend the anniversary, which we will talk about in chapter 12.

Keep in mind that this is part of your healing process. And you may want to honor your dog with a special celebration recounting your prized memories.

This first anniversary can bring new awareness to your healing journey and bring to the surface opportunities to move forward with your process.

Holidays, Birthdays & Special Days

Just like the first anniversary—holidays, birthdays, and special days that you spent with your dog can be excruciating and devastating to experience and/or remember.

For instance, holidays when you are supposed to be happy but you aren't can be super tough to navigate. When you observe everyone around you, smiling and celebrating, yet your heart is breaking, it can easily make you feel very alone with your loss.

If you are feeling this during a holiday celebration, the last thing you want to do is join in the merriment. It is okay if you don't. One of the most helpful tools that I share with my clients is to take a break.

The bathroom is the perfect place. If you feel as if you are going to cry, feel sad, or have anxiety or any other feelings of grief, you can go to the bathroom, shut the door, and have a moment to collect your thoughts and feelings before returning to a room full of people.

Piper did this a lot. It was a way for her to feel safe, take a breath, and remember Dandelion in peace. It was her special way to deal with holidays with a family that expected her to move quickly through her grief.

Birthdays are another tough time as are the anniversaries of special trips or events that you had with your dog. They act as triggers for your grief. They are reminders of your loss. Yet they can be excellent opportunities for helping you move to the next step of your journey, so you can make new choices and discover new ways of navigating your life.

There are many helpful ways to survive these days by paying tribute to your dog, which we will cover in chapters 12,13, and 15, with specific suggestions on how to create memorials and markers of time that demonstrate respect and caring for your dog.

Chapter Wrap-Up

In this chapter, we covered what to expect days, weeks, and years after the death of your beloved companion. By understanding the demands that our society places on our emotions and how we process them, you are reminded and encouraged to take the time you need to heal.

With the *Contemplation Questions* at the end of this chapter, you will take control of the time you need to experience your grief, and you will be ready to not be influenced by those around you to move faster.

In chapter 6, I am going to share ways to take care of yourself. I am going to give you reasons and examples of ways in which you can restore and support yourself during this painful and raw time.

Chapter 5 Contemplation Questions

In what ways are you feeling rushed with your grief journey? Who is rushing you?

What are you going to do to not rush your experience, to slow down and be where you are at? What are the ways you can be prepared if someone tries to rush you?

How have you spent, or are going to spend, the first anniversary of your dog's end of life? Write down the feelings of grief you are experiencing. If your dog has not been physically with you for years, how have you spent the anniversaries?

6. Taking Care of Yourself

When you experience the pain and shock of not having your dog with you 24/7, many things can happen to your well-being. By now you know that grief is a powerful force that has many personalities. It can change and affect your life in many ways. It can literally unhinge you from your daily life and zap your vitality.

However, allowing time for self-care in order to survive your loss is extremely helpful and important. Grief has a tendency to thrive when we are tired and at a loss. When we are rested, our chaotic minds are unable to overcome our senses.

While most of my clients feel guilty for resting and taking care of themselves during the period of initial loss, everyone needs downtime to heal and refresh. It is totally okay to do this. Not only is it okay, it is necessary. Self-care is actually a great way to manage your pet grief journey and allow greater focus, strength, and compassion to shine through.

Remember the free meditation that you downloaded in chapter 2? This meditation was created so that you can take a relaxing break to rejuvenate your soul. Please refer back to it to help you take care of yourself.

Case Study — Barbara and Noogett

After Noogett died, Barbara couldn't sleep. She forgot to eat and decided not to spend time with her friends. She didn't leave her house. In a very short period of time, she was completely exhausted and found herself with headaches and getting sick often.

What happened? Barbara stopped taking care of herself, and her resistance was low.

When Barbara reached out to me and we started to work together, we set up a self-care plan that she was comfortable with. As the weeks went by, Barbara stuck to her new plan and experienced some wonderful changes.

She found that as she became healthier, her grief was less intense, and she was able to visit her memories of her years with Noogett without feeling miserable. Plus, she was able to feel really good about some of the tough decisions that she'd had to make, which we will talk about more in the next section of this book.

The Best Advice

Now please listen closely to the best advice that I can give you right now and that I gave to Barbara—take some time for self-care right away. You may have been experiencing grief for a while or your grief may be new. It doesn't matter where you are in the grief journey; what matters is that you replenish your own body, mind, and soul.

The connection and your memories that you have with your dog will not go away if you take time to feel better. In fact, it will make your memories stronger and will help you heal during this terrible and devastating time.

If you are tired, burned out, stressed out, not eating, and not sleeping because your grief is so strong and you are feeling so incredibly alone, it will be difficult for you to make some important decisions. The last thing you want to do is make a decision that you will later regret.

Like Barbara, this is the time to take care of yourself so that you are functioning at the best you can and not relying on your reserves to get you through. Having strength is critical for you to be ready for the unexpected feelings of grief and how you are going to proceed with your new life.

The "What" of Self-Care

There are many things that you can do for yourself that don't cost a lot of money, like walking in nature, taking a nap, taking a bath, hanging out with friends, listening to relaxing music, or having a cup of tea.

Create a self-care plan that you would love to experience and that will give you the greatest support. Creating a successful self-care plan that includes some new activities as well as old activities that have already given you joy will ground you during this difficult time.

Remember, the healthier you are in body, mind, and spirit, the easier it is to cope and deal with the grief that you are going through. This is a tough period of loss no matter where you are in regards to the timeframe. Giving yourself some downtime will ease some of the pain and heal your grief as you continue your journey.

The Physical Self

Let's talk about some of the options for taking care of your physical body during this time. This is the time to put your grief on the shelf and just focus on you.

Your grief will have its chance to come back and challenge you, but for right now, this time is about you.

My clients find that when they do one or more of the following physical things for their bodies, they feel stronger and more in control of their grief. Even if they can do one of these things for only five to ten minutes a day, it still helps them in their journeys.

I suggest that you spend at least a half-hour every day if you can with any combination of the following activities for the health of your body, mind, and spirit:

- Massage

- Walks in nature

- Reiki or other forms of energy work

- Exercise class

- Nutritious and regular eating

- Plentiful sleep

- Short breaks throughout the day with your eyes closed

- Intentional and active breathing

If a half-hour every day is too much time, try to give yourself at least a half-hour three times a week during which you take care of your physical body.

The Mental Self

The next thing to take care of is your mind. As you know, your mind is going in a million different directions right now. Sometimes your mind clutter is creating so much anxiety and stress you wonder how you're going to manage.

To help your mind, you can find support groups, pet loss grief coaches, psychotherapists, friends, coworkers, family members, and veterinarians who respect the journey of pet grief you are going through. They should be there for you and be able to walk this journey with you so that you don't have to feel alone.

Finding ways to support your mind's health can take some time, yet if you know what you're looking for, the process can be less cumbersome.

Here are some other ways that you can create a healthy mind that can support you.

- Talk to a pet grief coach—a coach will listen and allow you to better manage your healing process.

- Talk to a psychotherapist or other health care provider—it is important to find someone that gets pet loss.

- Participate in pet loss support groups—these provide another way to support you. In them you will meet people that are going through similar situations. Be sure you find one where you feel that you are getting ample time to express your journey and are not being judged by anyone.

- Talk with select family and friends—this is a tough one. Your friends and family may mean well, yet they may also be the ones that trigger your grief because they really don't know how to support you. Choose wisely and choose only those friends and family that let you talk and that don't offer advice. Definitely stay away from the ones that judge you!

A healthy mind is a strong mind that creates balance when the mind clutter starts getting out of hand. Having a support system helps you monitor your mind and offers solutions when your grief is swirling out of control.

Choose a couple of these options that feel good to you. Do some research and don't feel bad if the person that you thought was your best friend doesn't support you. There is someone who will!

The Spiritual Self

Now let's talk about your spiritual health. Many times you can forget about this one when experiencing the newness of the death of your dog. You may even be uncomfortable with your spiritual beliefs or not have any.

Whatever your spiritual choice, remember, it is your journey. I encourage you to only incorporate a spiritual practice into your daily life if you feel comfortable doing so.

Here are some of the ways that you can create spiritual health in your life:

- Meditation comes in all forms. A quiet walk in the woods is equally meditative as is sitting quietly in one posture and clearing your mind of all thoughts.

- Yoga, tai chi, or other forms of spiritual-physical practice help your body become stronger. The discipline and focus create a connection to your inner spiritual force.

- Your spiritual practice, no matter what your belief is, and its daily, weekly, or periodic expression can help you receive solace.

- An animal medium or animal communicator is an excellent way to get peace of mind and learn the spiritual connection that you had with your dog from your dog's perspective. My clients that choose to have an animal mediumship session with me are greatly relieved to hear from their dogs again.

I have shared with you many ways to take care of yourself. It is totally up to you on how you would like to include one or many of the suggestions that I offered.

Remember, this is a trying time, and it can become very difficult as the days, weeks, and months progress. You are dealing with a huge shift in your daily life. Your pal is no longer physically present, and that is a lot to handle.

Creating a support team as we discussed is equally important as taking care of yourself. Being well rested, balanced, at peace are all the things you need to meet your grief head-on!

Use the three *Contemplation Questions* at the end of the chapter to take action for your own self-care without guilt. Even if the only thing you can do right now is simple breathing to create balance in your life, that is okay!

Chapter Wrap-Up

In this chapter, I shared ways that helped so many of my clients find peace of mind and strength after their dogs died. I encourage you to take some time for yourself without feeling guilty. Care for yourself in terms of your body, mind, and spirit.

By allowing time in your schedule for self-care, you will be able to move through your grief journey with more quality and awareness. You will make better decisions and be ready for unexpected grief too.

Remember to use the three *Contemplation Questions* to determine the what, when, and how of your own self-care.

In section 2, I am going to offer you support with some extremely difficult and sometimes painful decisions that you will be faced with and that need to be made.

Chapter 6 Contemplation Questions

How much time can you carve out for rejuvenating your soul, daily, weekly, and monthly?

How are you going to reach out to get support for your body and mind?

How are you going to support your spiritual beliefs? How are you going to practice your spiritual beliefs, so they directly support you with your emotions and stages of grief?

DECISIONS TO BE MADE: SECTION TWO

"Your pain is the breaking of the shell that encloses your understanding."

—Khalil Gibran

7. Caring for Your Dog's Body

Death happens to everyone, and we can't avoid it. By knowing and embracing your beliefs about hospice, the end of life, and the afterlife, your decision on how to care for your dog's body will empower you to feel great about the life that you had with your dog.

Death is something we can look at with respect, especially when making decisions and dealing with choices about what to do with the body of our beloved companion.

Remember that how you choose to care for your dog's body is your way of showing respect for yourself and the relationship you had with another living being. If you show over-the-moon love for your dog by choosing cremation, burial in your backyard, or burial in a pet cemetery (chapter 8) instead of letting your veterinarian take care of everything—that is absolutely okay. No one's judgment of you matters because it is you and your relationship with your dog that are at stake here.

I'm going to let you in on a little secret here—when you actively participate in deciding how to care for your dog's body, that nagging and painful grief feeling of guilt doesn't have much chance of surviving. Instead, by knowing how you are going to handle the body, making decisions, and taking an active role, you are going to win, and guilt will not have a chance.

I find in my practice mostly everybody, including myself, feels some level of guilt that we never did enough for our dogs. Know that this sentiment is common and universal.

Yet, when you take control, deciding how you are going to care for your dog's body in the most fitting way and how you will pay tribute to your dog, which we will cover in chapters 12 and 13, guilt cannot live in your heart. The only thing that continues to live in your heart is the love that you shared with your dog and the fact that you did the right thing.

Making sure that the body of your companion is handled perfectly is not weird. It shows courage, pride, and strength, all of which are incredibly powerful when experiencing the loss and grief that come with it.

The Pros and Cons

There are a few things to consider that can help you decide how to handle your dog's body.

When your veterinarian confronts you, asking, "What would you like to do with the body?" there are a couple of options for you to consider:

1. You can leave your dog with your veterinarian to take care of everything.

2. You can take your dog home to be buried or to a crematorium.

Either way or whatever your choice, there are pros and cons.

Option One: *You can leave your dog with your veterinarian to take care of everything.*

Option One Pros

If you let the vet do everything, it might help you process your grief in a way that makes sense to you. It might be too difficult for you to handle the body yourself and that is okay, so you should respect that in yourself.

Also, this might be the better choice if your dog died from an accident because seeing their body may be too painful for you to experience. It may trigger your grief to a point of not being healthy, and your memories of your dog would, therefore, be unpleasant and not something that you would like to remember.

Option One Cons

Once your veterinarian has the body, you do not know how the body of your dog is going to be handled. Many people don't want their dogs in a plastic bag, carried off to a back room, and then disposed of.

This is not to say that your veterinarian would be insensitive, but if you choose to let them be the caretakers, ask them to describe their protocol for handling their patients' bodies. You want to be sure this aligns with your beliefs. Total trust in your veterinarian is paramount.

Another con is that if your dog died at home in their sleep, for instance, it might seem strange or awkward for you to take their body to the veterinarian's office. It might be less stressful or traumatic if you keep their body at home for a possible backyard burial, or you call a crematorium of choice to make arrangements. (Both of these options we'll be discussing in detail in chapter 8.)

The biggest disadvantage with leaving your dog's body with the vet is that you don't have control and you don't know if your dog is being treated with respect.

Option Two: *You can take your dog home to be buried or to a crematorium.*

Option Two Pros

If you are able to make the choice of being able to take control of your dog's body and not have your veterinarian do it, I would highly suggest this option.

I recommend this option for the reason that you get to fully control how your dog's body is being handled, which can give you a sense of healthy closure, just as it did for Martha whose story I'm about to share to demonstrate this pro.

Case Study — Martha and Teddy

Teddy had a difficult final six months of life. In the end, Martha made a frantic call to the veterinarian who put Teddy down as Martha held him—there was no time for a sedative because he was in such pain. Martha barely had time to really say good-bye. She was majorly traumatized, as was he.

The day Teddy died, Martha knew she wanted to be the one to care for Teddy's body and not let the veterinarian take him. It was her way of processing and letting go as she dealt with his last days of suffering and his abrupt ending.

Martha could not bear to have anyone else handle Teddy's body. It was very important to her that his body was handled properly. So what happened was that two of Martha's girlfriends drove her, with Teddy's body in the back of the car, to a crematorium.

The crematorium had a special service where they made a paw print in plaster before they cremated Teddy's body. Martha keeps that plastered paw print and Teddy's ashes on her living room shelf.

Additionally, Martha feels so fortunate to have had her friends be with her in that emergency situation. It meant the world to her.

* * *

Here is what happens with this choice—you get to deal with your loss on another level, one that allows you to actively participate, possibly even have friends help you, all so you can learn about your relationship with your dog in an entirely different way. When you actively participate, a new form of love fills your heart that is directly associated with your dog and your healing.

It also allows you additional time for closure. For example, another client of mine, Susanne, decided that she was going to take Trixie to the crematorium herself. On her way there, she opened all the car windows so that Trixie could feel the air on her body one last time. This gave Susanne an extra boost of joy, and she often recalled this memory when she was feeling alone.

Plus, it was Susanne's way of saying good-bye to Trixie. Saying good-bye is equally important and appropriate, no matter what your choices are. It is another way of respecting and honoring the relationship that you had with your dog.

This is not to say that you won't experience grief, but what it will give you is memories and a sense that you did everything you could for your dog.

Option Two Cons

Sometimes when you choose to deal with your dog's body, it can be an overwhelming experience to drive your dog home to be buried or to the crematorium.

If you have children at home (something we'll explore in chapter 9) or unsupportive family members, it could make the experience of handling your dog's body yourself difficult or unpleasant for you.

The other thing to think about is that if you want to bury your dog in your backyard, the season will factor into the decision. If the ground is frozen, it is difficult to do a backyard burial. If this is the case, you'll want to have a plan on how you are going to preserve the body.

For example, my clients Susan and Fred wanted a backyard burial, so they brought Angus home, put him in the freezer, and waited until spring. This may sound gruesome to some, but to Susan and Fred, it was what they wanted to do for Angus. Doing so helped them process their grief.

Here are some other potential difficulties to consider too:

- You may not have a pet crematorium in your area, and it would be difficult for you to transport your dog's body to a crematorium in another part of the state or even to a whole different state.

- If you live in an apartment building, you may not have land for a burial.

- The cost of either cremation or burial in a pet cemetery could be prohibitive, so other possibilities would need to be considered.

No matter what your choice is for the handling of your dog's body, keep in mind that it is your choice and you make your decision based on your beliefs, needs, and desires.

Chapter Wrap-Up

In this chapter, I supplied you with information and considerations to help with the decision on how you would like to handle your dog's body. There are many ways to look at this personal choice. The key is to understand what you can handle, what you want to deal with, and what is going to help you feel better.

With the chapters three *Contemplation Questions*, you will explore your own personal beliefs and feelings in order to arrive at the most appropriate decision for you and your dog.

In chapter 8, we are going to talk about the particular variables at play in regards to deciding between a backyard burial, a cremation, or a pet cemetery burial for your beloved companion. You will learn about the details of each option and explore which is the best for you.

Chapter 7 Contemplation Questions

Do you want your vet to take care of everything? If so, why is that right for you, and how are you going to say good-bye? List the pros and cons that are unique to this choice for you.

Do you want to take care of your dog's body yourself? List the pros and cons about this decision for you.

Just as Susanne lowered the windows of her car while driving Trixie's body to the crematorium, consider a final symbolic gesture that you could do to demonstrate love and respect for your furry pal. Make sure the gesture complements the decision you've made to either ask your vet to handle your dog's body or to handle it yourself.

8. Choosing Burial, Cremation, or Pet Cemetery

For those of you who made the decision not to leave your dog's body with the veterinarian, in this chapter we are going to explore options for handling your dog's remains either through cremation or burial.

The Cremation Option

Many of my clients choose cremation over burial. Everyone has their own unique reasons, but the two most prevalent reasons for cremation are (1) city ordinances in urban communities and (2) they want the ashes of their dog, so they can keep them or sprinkle them in a favorite place as a formal way of saying good-bye.

Case Study — Pam and Mergie

My client Pam, an avid traveler, went everywhere with her dog Mergie. She and Mergie would take a yearly trip from New Hampshire to Sedona, Arizona, to hike and rest.

Pam knew that when Mergie died, she would be taking a road trip without Mergie for the sole purpose of sprinkling her ashes around the country, and one of those places would be the Southwest.

One of her favorite places to go was Sedona, Arizona. Mergie and Pam would spend every day hiking to a new spot to enjoy the healing energy of this beautiful landscape.

When she arrived in Sedona with Mergie's ashes, Pam picked a favorite hiking spot each day there and said a little prayer while sprinkling Mergie's ashes during the hikes to say good-bye.

After her return home, Pam shared with me, "I am so happy I took this trip with Mergie's ashes. I felt her spirit with me the entire time. I loved that I took control and planned for us to have a road trip again. It was so healing for me. Being able to say good-bye in this way helped me feel Mergie in my heart even more."

Pam is not alone when it comes to choosing cremation. Debi shared this story about her little bundle of sweetness named Niko:

> *"On Niko's last night, I told him that I'd be having him cremated, so he could always be with me. I explained that I was going to share his ashes with his grandparents, so he could always be with them too, and that I was getting two more small urns—a heart necklace to keep him near my heart every day and a key chain, so he could go with me everywhere because he loved going for rides in my truck."*

This option is becoming more and more popular. Since cremation has become more popular, more options are available for you to choose from.

I recommend that you ask your veterinarian which crematorium they use and then make sure to do your own research. You want to be sure you choose a place that has strict ethics and spotless business practices.

How Cremation Works

Your pet is placed in a chamber that is heated between 1400 and 1800 degrees. The heat reduces your pet's remains to basic calcium compounds. In other words, to ashes.

After these ashes cool, they are removed from the chamber and placed in an urn or a container of your choice. You are then able to take them home and keep them with you.

Types of Cremation

Please keep in mind there are different types of cremations for dogs.

The first is a *private cremation*. This is one in which your dog will be alone in the cremation chamber, and you will receive the ashes of your dog alone. This option is the most expensive, and exact fees depend on your geographical area.

The second option is a *viewing cremation*, which is not always available. It is the same as a private cremation but also allows family to be present during the process in a separate viewing room. This option, if available, is less expensive than the private cremation but can have a considerable cost associated with it.

The third option is a *semi-private* or *partitioned cremation*, which allows for multiple pets in the same chamber. Your dog would have their own partition; however, the ashes that you receive would be from all the pets in that chamber, not just your dog's. This alternative is not as expensive as the private cremation but is more costly than the final option.

Please note that this process can also be considered a private cremation at some facilities. I always remind to my clients that they clarify the particularities with the facility they use— and you should do the same. You don't want to risk your dog's ashes mixing with others if that is not what you want or expect.

The final option is a *communal cremation*, which is also known as a *mass* or *batch cremation*. This form of service places multiple animals in the same chamber with no form of separation. No ashes are returned to you. This is the least expensive type of cremation.

Keep in mind that various facilities will have different ways of explaining their services. Again—please ask questions and get clarification if there is something you do not understand.

Personally, I visited two pet crematoriums in my area and asked to see the facilities as well as descriptions of their services. The folks that ran both of these facilities were very compassionate people and offered other services as well, such as a paw print in plaster, a lock of fur, beautiful urn choices, and an honoring of the request to have a favorite toy or blanket in the chamber.

When I work with my clients on deciding about cremation, there are some common questions that come up that I would like to share with you. It is understandable you would have questions and concerns surrounding your pet's aftercare.

I stress to my clients that no matter whom you choose to perform this service, be sure to ask the following questions.

Also, be a hundred percent satisfied with the answers before you move forward.

Essential Questions to Ask Crematorium Facilities

1. *Who exactly will perform the cremation?*

You want to make sure the person handling your dog and handling the cremation furnace is a person of integrity who is experienced at the work—not someone who is unskilled, untrained, overworked, or hates their job. Basically, the pet crematorium industry is not highly regulated at this time, so be prepared to ask them lots of questions about their practices.

2. *How long will I have to wait for the cremation to take place?*

This varies from facility to facility. Some cremations take several weeks; some take several days. The reason for this is that they may be busy with other cremations or only schedule pets on certain days. Make sure you ask them or get an answer from your veterinarian if you leave your dog with them.

In my experience, if it takes several days or weeks, you can leave the body at the crematorium. They are equipped for this, and if the facility has high standards, it will take very good care of your dog's body. Again, find out how the body will be cared for in the event you have to wait.

I personally choose a crematorium where I can wait for my dog's ashes. This way I feel more secure, safe, and at peace.

Knowing how long it will take will help you with your stress level and, therefore, not trigger your grief.

3. *How do I know that the ashes I am receiving are my dog's?*

Whether you allow your veterinarian full control or you take your dog's body to the crematorium, ask them how they keep track of the animal remains at their facility. If you don't like the answer, move on. If you do like the response and you trust the individual or organization's answer, this can provide you with peace of mind.

Home Burial

If cremation is not your choice, there is also the option of a home burial. This allows you to bury your pup at home. If you live in an urban area, this might not be allowed, so check that out first. However, if you live in the country, you may opt for a home burial so that you can bury your beloved companion in their favorite spot.

Keep in mind though there are some practical and some difficult things you will encounter and must consider when burying your dog.

It is important to choose your gravesite carefully. Some of my clients pick areas that they loved or that their dogs loved, such as a sunny spot near a tree.

You will want to choose a place that will not be disturbed in the future. Don't put your dog's gravesite in a wet area, near cables or underground pipes, or even near water sources, such as wells, ponds, and streams. You want an undisturbed, dry area that will be a permanent place for you to visit.

Also consider the size of the gravesite. You will need to dig at least four to five feet down into the ground. This will ensure that other animals will not disturb the burial area, or rain will not wash the topsoil away and expose the grave, which could be a very traumatic experience for you.

I also encourage my clients to bury their dogs in something that is biodegradable rather than plastic—towels, wood, and cloth are great choices. Try to stay away from plastic caskets or burying them with their favorite bed if it was stuffed with synthetic material.

My clients who choose this option place a stone or a marker at the site, which is a great way to memorialize your dog (we will talk about this more in chapter 12). It also lends to the sacredness of the site.

Pet Cemetery

One of the reasons why you may like to choose a pet cemetery is that if you do a home burial, you may not live at your current home for your entire life. This would mean that if you move, you will not be able to take the body of your pet with you.

For this reason, a pet cemetery would provide you with a sacred site to visit and remember your companion.

When choosing a pet cemetery, there are many things to consider. First, be sure that the cemetery that you choose is a current member of the International Association of Pet Cemeteries and Crematoriums (IAOPCC.) Go to their website and be sure they are a current member.

Unlike human cemeteries, pet cemeteries are not regulated in all states. So be aware of the standards and laws in your individual state.

Things to ask include the following:

1. Who owns the land where the facility is?

2. Are you running out of land for burials?

3. Are there any deed restrictions?

4. Will this land ever be used for something else?

5. How long have you been established?

6. Who owns the facility?

7. Are you a member of the IAOPCC?

8. Who are the employees, and what is their experience?

9. What are the fees?

The other thing to consider is who is going to take your dog to the cemetery. Many cemeteries offer this service as does your veterinarian's office. Your decision will be based on trusting your choice and whether you are emotionally able to transport your dog.

In my experience, every pet cemetery is different in the way that they provide services for their clients. Price ranges vary according to location.

The best thing to do is find a pet cemetery in your area that is registered with the IAOPCC and ask the questions that I gave you above. Make sure they are trusted and a well-respected business.

Then if you are happy with their answers, you can go a step further and ask them specific questions about costs, etc.

Here are some things to consider when speaking to the staff at the pet cemetery of your choice:

1. What are my choices and prices for the gravesite of my dog?

2. Do you offer transportation of my dog's body from my home or from my veterinarian's office?

3. Do you offer individual plots or are your plots communal?

4. Who takes care of the general maintenance of my dog's gravesite? Are there extra fees?

5. Am I allowed to come visit the gravesite whenever I want?

6. Do you offer funeral services?

7. Can I leave toys at my dog's gravesite?

Pet cemeteries can provide you with caskets, headstones, and burial site maintenance. Just be clear and prepared if you go with this option about all the costs involved.

As a pet funeral celebrant, I have been asked to lead various pet funerals and memorial services in some amazing pet cemeteries that were beautifully cared for and maintained. Yet, there have been some that I questioned. Do your research and be sure the pet cemetery of your choice meets your criteria.

Chapter Wrap-Up

In this chapter, you learned of ways that you can respectfully take care of your dog's body. You learned how to research a crematorium and about the cremation process. You also have some questions to ask when considering a crematorium. If cremation is not your choice, you learned of two burial options that may suit your needs instead, as well as important considerations for each of these.

With the *Contemplation Questions* at the end of this chapter, you will get a chance to explore how you feel about cremation or burial to help you become clearer about your choice.

Chapter 9 will be helpful to you if you have children of your own or if there were children in your dog's life that will miss your dog. While death in our society can be a difficult topic for adults, teaching a child about pet loss is important for building honesty and resilience.

Chapter 8 Contemplation Questions

Are you trying to decide between cremation or burial? Do some research that will help you decide. Research the crematorium and pet cemetery options in your area. Also, find out about your locality's rules on burying pets at home.

How do you feel about cremation? If you choose cremation, what questions would you ask your veterinarian and/or crematorium?

Have you considered a home burial? If so, where would that be? How would you mark the gravesite?

9. Helping Children with Pet Loss

In our society death is a very difficult topic, and for the most part we would all like to avoid it. Yet, death is part of life. When teaching your child about pet loss, it is important to know your feelings and attitudes about death first. If you are unclear about these, your confused or vague explanation of death could, in turn, affect the way your child views loss in the future.

As an adult, you know there is an end to all life. The thing to remember is that even though you understand that all living things die, the death of your dog may be the first time your child, or a child in your dog's life, encounters death. What this means is that your child will likely experience new, and perhaps difficult, feelings.

Since children are naturally curious and want to know how things work, they will experience various stages of grief and loss that could be extremely difficult for them to comprehend. However, this could be the perfect opportunity to teach them about life and death, and help them be more resilient as they age.

Guidelines for Supporting a Child

Your child will look to you to help them through their feelings of grief, mourning, and understanding that death is normal. There are many ways that you can help your child understand the loss of their pet.

These five tips are the guidelines that I use with my clients when they are looking for additional support with children. In using these five tips, you will create a very healthy and positive atmosphere and experience for your child.

Tip 1—*Honesty is critical when talking about death to your child.*

If you are unclear about your feelings about death, it will be difficult to be honest. However, it is important to tell your child the truth. Avoid half-truths, generalizations, or the use of clichés or myths (chapter 3).

Your child will ask you questions about where their pet went, whether their pet will come back, and why the death happened. By answering with clear and informative responses, you will help them to develop a healthy attitude.

It is important to tell them that their pet has not gone to sleep, run away, or is living on a farm. Depending on the age of your child, you will be crafting your response according to their level of development.

Be clear, honest, and talk about death in simple and specific terms.

For example, if your child is five years old or younger, you could say, "Max died. His body just stopped working. He has stopped eating, moving, seeing, and hearing. We are all going to miss him."

This was exactly what my clients Tim and Carol told their child Emily when Max died. They did it this way to lessen her fear. They had to tell Emily this over and over, but it helped Emily understand that her pal died. It didn't scare her or create myths or untruths about life and death.

By eight or nine, children are able to grasp the meaning of death, so it will be appropriate to explain it in more adult terms. Knowing how you feel about death and the grieving process will help you craft meaningful explanations for your child.

For example, Robin told her son Travis the following when he asked how long Mecco was going to live:

> *"Mecco's body hurts, and he is very old. Mecco has trouble eating, so he is not getting the nutrients he needs. His tumor is making him very sick. So instead of letting him suffer any longer, it is time to let him die. Remember, how I explained that to you? We will take Mecco to the vet, and the vet will give him medication that will help him do this."*

Tip 2—*Carefully allow your emotions of grief to show in front of your child.*

As you know, full honesty is important when explaining death to your child. Even still, keep in mind that since the emotions of grief may be new for your child, when they observe your emotions, this experience will affect them.

When your emotions are heightened, it is okay to share them with your child. You loved the family pet, and your emotions are important to express and understand. Depending on the age of your child, the death of their pet is going to bring on feelings that they have not experienced before.

Your feelings of grief, such as crying and being sad, are normal when losing a beloved dog and are important to share. When you show these feelings to your child, it will help them understand that their feelings are normal too. Yet, if you become raging with anger or extremely depressed, those emotions may not be healthy for your child to experience at this time. Extreme emotions of grief are better to express without your child observing.

Robin oftentimes had to go into her bedroom to express her extreme crying when Travis was home from school. She felt that sometimes her pain was just too raw for Travis to observe and would only frighten him. However, when she expressed her sadness in front of Travis, she felt comfortable with gentle tears and expression.

Tip 3—*Help, guide, and support your child through their feelings of grief.*

Once you know and understand what the common feelings of grief are (chapters 1 and 2), share them with your child and allow your child to talk about them with you. Your child will probably have many questions, so be prepared to talk to them and explain to them what happens during the end-of-life period.

Robin did this with Travis. She took the list in this book and showed it to Travis. They talked about each item on the list and how it made them feel. She answered Travis' questions and let him know that his feelings are important.

Tip 4—*Grief and mourning are different.*

When you create the time for your child to ask questions and express their grief, it will provide a time for you and your family to lovingly create another level of closeness and bonding. Grief is an inward expression of suffering from a loss, and mourning is the outward expression (more in chapter 11). It is so important to allow them to outwardly express their inner grief with a pet funeral or pet memorial that they design.

When your child can express their ideas, thoughts, and suggestions, they will know that you support them fully. It will help them with their feelings of grief, teach them about losses in life, and help them to develop into adaptable and functional adults.

In chapter 12, we will talk about how to create life celebrations that will help not only you but also your child to have a healthy experience participating in this part of life with their pet.

Tip 5—*Be an example for how to move through the grieving process.*

Since the death of your child's pet may be the first experience your child will have surrounding death and grief, understanding your own reactions is critical.

There are many myths that surround death that we covered in chapter 3. When you explore these myths, they can help you understand and process your feelings. Also, understanding that grief has a life of its own that can surface at unexpected times will help you be prepared for your child's question, fears, and feelings.

Knowing what normal grief is as opposed to abnormal grief will guide you to a clearer perspective so that you can be fully aware and present for your child during this difficult time (chapters 1 and 2).

Since this is the first exposure to death that your child may be experiencing, know that they probably will not know how to respond or why they have the feelings that they do.

This experience gives you the opportunity to be a confidant, teacher, supporter, and role model who is there for them, listens, and unconditionally loves them, just as their pet did.

Chapter Wrap-Up

In this chapter you learned why pets are so important and how they can be incredible teachers for introducing death to your child. With the five tips provided, you will be able to support your child in their first encounter with death and be the perfect role model for this life experience.

With the chapter's *Contemplation Questions* below, you will begin to organize your plan of action on how to help your child.

In the next chapter, you will explore a very common issue concerning the right time to get another dog. Most of my clients go through varying levels of anguish about inviting another dog into their lives after the deaths of their beloved companions. You will hear my story about Addie, as well as Sandy's, Ralph's, and Trisha's stories. Plus, you will receive eight tips to help you with this decision.

Chapter 9 Contemplation Questions

What are your feelings about death? Can you make a list? Do you consider each of your feelings about death healthy?

How will you tell your child about death when they ask you about the death of their pet?

Are there any comments that you made that may be half-true, vague, or considered to be a myth? If so, can you change them to reflect a clear and honest answer?

10. Getting Another Dog?

Determining when to get another dog can be an excruciating decision for you. This decision oftentimes has people going back and forth, never seeming to reach a decision they feel a hundred percent confident about.

Unfortunately, the loss of our dogs is inescapable since their lifespans are not as long as ours. Still, it doesn't lessen the pain of loss in any way. Your grief is still going to be felt, and you are going to feel alone if you don't have other critters in your household.

For some of my clients, opening their heart to a new dog to invite into their home right after their companion dies is extremely helpful. Yet for other clients, it can take a long time before they are ready. For others, they never are able to have another dog because the pain is so intense.

Remember in chapters 1 and 2 when I talked about how grief has a life of its own? How grief is unique to you and everyone is different with how they process their grief? Similarly, making a decision to get another dog is a personal choice for you to make.

My clients Sandy and Ralph couldn't imagine a home without a dog, and they remedied it very quickly after Sophia died. They couldn't stand coming home and not having the comforting sound of Sophia running towards them, welcoming them home. To Sandy and Ralph, getting a new dog quickly eased their sadness and brought joy. For them, it was the right choice.

Yet my client Trisha needed to grieve her loss of Boomer much longer before she felt it was appropriate to adopt another dog. She felt that she needed time alone with her grief so that she could work through her feelings without having a new dog to distract her.

For her, this was the sensible thing to do because she wanted to be sure that she didn't "replace" Boomer. She also didn't want to feel disloyal to Boomer by opening her heart to another dog.

While some people are like Sandy and Ralph and want a new dog right away and other people are like Trisha and want to wait a long time, there are others that have no timeframe at all. They make the choice to wait until the right dog comes along—just as my husband Rick and I did after Marley died.

Sharing My Story

If you read *My Dog Is Dying: What Do I Do?,* you already know the story of how Marley died. If you did not read it, let me share that our beautiful dog Marley died from nasosarcoma. It was tragic and horrible to lose such a beautiful dog to such an angry disease.

After she died, both Rick and I knew we were going to get another dog, yet we didn't know when. We chose to wait until the time was right.

As an animal communicator, I tend to wait for a sign, if you will, that will guide me to the right decision. When it comes to choosing animals, I wait for what I call the "heart-melt." I am sure you know what I am talking about.

The "heart-melt" is when you hold a dog, and both hearts just seem to melt together. When we met Addie from the humane society, we had no intention that day to adopt. We were just helping out with the first plane rescue at our local shelter.

When Addie came off the plane, I stepped up to take her from the woman handing out puppies. I took her to put her in a crate. Well, you can probably imagine—I had a "heart-melt." Addie just mushed into my heart, giving my husband and me licks, and we came home with a beautiful puppy.

I knew that it was the right time, and by inviting Addie into our lives, I wasn't disrespecting Marley in any way. In fact, Marley prepared our hearts for this beautiful baby.

Most of my clients go through varying levels of anguish about inviting another dog into their lives after the deaths of their beloved companions. It is a very common feeling, and it is normal. By hearing my story as well as Sandy's, Ralph's, and Trisha's, I hope you will be able to trust where you are at with your journey of grief to make the best decision for you.

Things to Keep in Mind

1. When welcoming another dog into your family, no matter where you are with your grief, this action can trigger feelings of loss that you thought you had already dealt with. It can challenge you to deal with them on a deeper level, which can be uncomfortable, surprising, and uninvited.

2. There is no right or wrong time to bring another dog into your life. It's really up to you. There are some things to consider to be sure that you are truly ready, but there are no hard-and-fast rules for making this decision.

3. Try not to make a hasty decision. Give yourself time to grieve and think. Don't let anyone tell you what the right decision is or pressure you into getting a dog.

4. Your new dog should not be considered a "replacement" for your previous dog. Replacement relationships are not healthy, and when you build a new relationship with a new dog, your memories and experiences will be different, unique, and very special to the two of you.

5. It is important to involve all family members in the decision to invite a new dog into the household. In particular, consider the needs and feelings of your children. They can easily feel that having a new pet in the home can be disloyal to the previous dog. Everyone in the family needs to have their chance to properly grieve.

6. Since your new dog begins a new relationship with you, it can be very difficult to heal your grief by naming the new dog the same as your previous dog's name. Try and come up with a new name that reflects the personality of your dog and their special antics, personality, etc.

7. Having the expectation that your new dog will learn, do, respond, or have the same characteristics as your previous dog is not respectful to your new dog. As an alternative, enjoy your new dog as a unique character with a ton of love, fun, and enjoyment to give you. Be excited by the differences and quirkiness.

8. If you have other pets in the house, consider if they might enjoy or resent a new dog. Some dogs will mourn the loss of their companion, so it will be important for their health and well-being to support the grief of the surviving dog.

Similarly, to the case studies in this chapter and the *Things to Keep in Mind* that I listed above, whether or not to get a new dog really depends on how comfortable you are with the stage of grief that you are in (chapter 2) and if you feel that your grief no longer affects the way you experience your daily life.

When my clients tell me they were at the humane society and found the perfect dog, yet they question if the time is right, I remind them to step back, take a breath, and trust what they are feeling in their hearts, just as I did with Addie. If there is confusion or doubt, it may mean they are still not ready, and that is okay. But, if the "heart-melt" overcomes the uncertainty, then this may be the perfect time.

Finally, if you are not convinced that you are ready for a new dog, there is always the option to volunteer at your humane society or local rescue group. You would be able to spend time cuddling, socializing, and maybe even fostering a dog in need. You will be able to share the love in your heart and receive comfort in knowing that you are doing something good. This is an excellent way to discover your new companion when you least expect it—just as Addie and I did!

Chapter Wrap-Up

In this chapter, you learned how to explore and feel confident about when you are ready to bring another dog into your home. You understand the importance of knowing where you are in your stages of grief and how this can affect your decision. Plus, you received eight *Things To Consider* when contemplating your decision.

You heard my story about adopting Addie and the stories of Sandy, Ralph, and Trisha, and how they became familiar with their nuances of grief to determine the right time to get another dog.

With the three *Contemplation Questions*, you will be able to begin the process of knowing when you are ready to bring another dog into your life and how you will go about finding your "heart-melt" dog!

In the next chapter, you are going to begin exploring the topic of ways to celebrate the life you had with your dog. We will begin in chapter 11 by exploring the difference between "grief" and "mourning."

Chapter 10 Contemplation Questions

Are you ready to get another dog now? If so, list the reasons why. After making your list, do you still feel like you are ready?

If you are not ready to welcome another dog into your life now, can you list the reasons why? Can you change those reasons into positive statements that help you process your feelings of grief?

How do you see your process of inviting another dog into your home unfolding? What does that look like? Will you rescue, foster, volunteer, or something else?

CELEBRATIONS OF LIFE FOR HEALING: SECTION THREE

"Grief is in two parts. The first is loss. The second is the remaking of life."

—Anne Roiphe

11. Starting to Mourn

For many of us, the words "grief" and "mourning" have been used interchangeably to mean the same thing. However, they are quite different. Knowing that difference will help you with your own journey of healing your grief over losing your furry companion.

As you learned in chapters 1 and 2, grief is your emotional reaction or physical response to your unique loss. Grief can be experienced as shock, confusion, anger, depression, sadness, anxiety, and more.

If you allow your grief to be felt and you accept that grief is normal, your journey to peace gradually changes. Your grief is your body's way of dealing with an event that you may not be able to fully process in that moment. It takes time for your soul to process grief, so please be patient with yourself.

If the death of your dog was sudden or totally unexpected, your struggle may take some time to completely understand. Whereas, if your dog was ill and dying for a while, the time that you need to process your grief is a very different experience.

The important thing to remember is that the loss of your dog is not entirely about losing your companion that you love dearly. It takes into consideration your dreams of what you hold precious and endearing to everyday life. For this reason, it is crucial that you give yourself "permission" to feel your loss and give yourself the space to heal your heart.

Case Study — Veronica and Cracker

Veronica found that with the loss of her dog Cracker it was much easier to survive her grief by not pushing her feelings away. Veronica told me, "I tried to bury my emotions, but I could never get peace. Even when I thought they went away, they would rise up and remind me of the pain I felt. When I understood this and felt comfortable expressing my grief, it finally started to feel like my feelings had a voice to express."

For Veronica, she talked about the pain of Cracker's death to a supportive friend and during our weekly calls. She kept talking and feeling. She sought out people in her daily life that would allow her to feel bad, feel guilty, and feel angry. She fully participated in her mourning period by sharing her feelings with those that did not judge her.

* * *

Keep in mind that your grief could get derailed if someone gives you a timeline of expectations. "You should be better by now. It has been six months" or "Why are you still feeling so guilty?" If you listen to these statements, as well as the other myths from chapter 3, you may not have the necessary time to mourn and get distracted from your journey. Veronica, in her "hunt" for supportive people, quickly learned how to include select people in her grief journey (and exclude others!).

Your journey will vary and be different from anyone else's. The pressure to "get better quickly" is one to stay away from.

It will ultimately guide you to the opposite of the peace that you may be seeking. Feelings do take a while to process.

You will probably never completely lose your feeling of sadness about the loss of your dog, but with time, the frequency and intensity will change. In fact, by allowing your grief to speak and express itself as a remedy for your pain, your healing will come about in time.

On Mourning

The mourning of your dog is the next step. You may not feel like it makes any sense right now, or you may feel that it is impossible for you to go to this next step; however, mourning is a very beautiful and sacred time for you.

You learned that grief is the internal expression of losing your dog. Mourning is the opposite. It is the outward expression of your grief. We can go deeper and say that mourning is the process that you choose to undertake in order to cope with the intense void that you are experiencing.

When you are ready to mourn, the reflection and introspection of the life you shared with your dog can be very strong and profound. It is the time to love even more deeply and remember that sweet and endearing love that you shared with your dog that you deeply miss.

This experience will help you as you begin to create a celebration of your dog's life (chapter 12) and while you start to anticipate the changes in your own life (chapter 14).

Remembering, expressing, and being open to developing a new clarity will allow you to gain insight into and empathy for your new life. Although this time can be extremely painful and difficult, your grief and mourning process can reveal some amazing gifts that aid you in understanding who you are. Your dog was a patient and loving teacher. This is the time period to fully reflect on those lessons.

Like grieving, mourning can be a difficult time. Yet, both are necessary for healing pet loss. By walking the journey of pet loss grief and creating a special ceremony that honors the life you had with your pet, you can learn so much and gain a tremendous gift from the experience.

Your animal devoted themselves to you and you to them. The physical loss of that deserves to be mourned. Managing your grief through this period can give you some amazing insight in relation to what your bond truly meant.

Chapter Wrap-Up

In this chapter, you learned that both grief and mourning have different roles in your journey of healing the loss of your beloved four-legged companion. Even though they can overlap and have no timeframe, your outward expression of your grief (i.e., mourning) will be an invaluable learning tool and a beautiful, sacred time.

With the chapter's *Contemplation Questions*, you will reflect on your own mourning experience and discover how mourning is actually the remedy to heal your pain.

In chapter 12, you will learn of actual ways to express your grief through some mourning rituals. When you are ready to approach healing your pet loss with a pet funeral, pet memorial, pet remembrance, and/or an end-of-life celebration, chapter 12 will guide you.

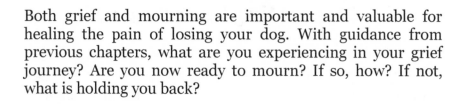

Chapter 11 Contemplation Questions

Both grief and mourning are important and valuable for healing the pain of losing your dog. With guidance from previous chapters, what are you experiencing in your grief journey? Are you now ready to mourn? If so, how? If not, what is holding you back?

How can mourning heal your body, mind, and spirit?

Can you list ways that you will be compassionate and patient with yourself during your mourning?

12. Celebrating Your Dog's Life

Grief is different from mourning, and you can easily get caught up with your grief and forget to outwardly express your feelings. Learning how to express your grief and mourn the loss of your dog is an important step when healing your pet loss. Mourning is a way of saying good-bye in a very healthy way.

In this chapter, you are going to explore the different ways in which you will both mourn and celebrate your dog's life—through a pet funeral or other type of end-of-life celebration. If you are ready for something different yet extremely beneficial for your heart and soul, the celebrations that I am going to share with you in this chapter provide new ways of respecting and honoring your dog.

Since you are a very special person that wants to honor your dog, please remember that if someone tells you that you are weird for holding an end-of-life ceremony for your dog— PLEASE DON'T LISTEN! If you listen, you will be holding back a very important step for healing your grief.

By going through the creative and necessary process of mourning (chapter 11) and exploring the options in this chapter, you will have the chance to respectfully celebrate the life of your dog and thank them for everything they did for you.

Also, by spending time creating your own end-of-life ceremony or by having a pet funeral celebrant help you create a personalized celebration, you will get the chance to have some closure and say good-bye. I have been conducting pet funerals and pet memorials for many years, and I have found that the value of holding a commemorative event is an invaluable aid in the healing process. Expressing your feelings and showing tribute to your dog is healthy, normal, and essential.

Case Study — Jeremy, Annie & Oscar

My clients Jeremy and Annie hired me to conduct an elegant celebration when their dog Oscar was buried in their backyard. I worked with them to compose a beautiful eulogy that paid tribute to all the things that they shared with Oscar.

They invited friends and family that loved Oscar as they did, and they even had some of Oscar's best four-legged buddies attend as well.

It was a beautiful day, the sun was warm, and there was a light breeze. When I read the eulogy, there were tears and smiles demonstrating the love and support for the relationship that Jeremy and Annie had with Oscar.

After the ceremony Annie told me in private, "Wendy, this was absolutely perfect. I am so glad we had a funeral for Oscar. I could feel him sitting by my side enjoying his tribute. I feel so complete, so healed. I know I will still feel grief, but I also have this beautiful memory that I celebrated the life we shared with him."

Let me share with you Oscar's eulogy.

Eulogy for Oscar

Hello, everyone. As many of you know, Oscar was the high-spirited dog that was adopted from a shelter many years ago. Annie and Jeremy have asked me to share with you a few stories as we remember what a great companion Oscar was to his family.

When Oscar first came home with Annie and Jeremy, he was totally obsessed with tennis balls. He would steal them from other dogs at the dog park. He could not walk by an active tennis court without trying to go in and get all the balls that he could! He did not care if it was new or old, purple, yellow, or green . . . chewed up or not. He loved any and all tennis balls. One could say he was obsessed with them.

Yet, after a few months, that all changed once he came to live with Annie and Jeremy. He gave up the obsession with tennis balls and, instead, decided to focus all of his obsessive energy on both of them. As long as Oscar could see Annie and Jeremy, all was good. Heaven forbid they would go behind closed doors for even a second or go into a different room . . . Oscar would jump off whatever comfortable chair he was on and FOLLOW either one of them like their own personal shadow! Up the stairs, down the stairs, into the bathroom, into the bedroom, and all over, Oscar had to keep either of them within constant eyesight!

Even as Oscar got older, Annie and Jeremy became his whole world. He would wait for them to settle down to watch the evening news, and he would curl up beside them, chin on Jeremy or Annie's lap, and fall asleep. It was his favorite time of day. And theirs, too. Anyone who had the opportunity to witness the devotion that Oscar had for Jeremy and Annie knew it was the unconditional love that a dog has for its family.

Thank you, Oscar, for being there for Annie and Jeremy, and being their constant companion. You were an angel disguised as a brown-and-white, fluffy dog!

Types of Celebrations

Here are some definitions of the types of end-of-life celebrations that you can consider when you are ready for this step in healing your pet loss. I listed them here and will talk more about them later in this chapter

Pet Funeral—This is a celebration/service in which the body or cremains of your pet are present. This event takes place relatively soon after your pet reaches the end of their life.

Pet Memorial—This is the celebration/service in which the body or cremains of your pet are not present. This event can take place whenever you so choose. There is no time limit as to when a pet memorial takes place.

Pet Remembrances—These are the anniversaries, holidays, and/or special occasions that you shared with your pet during which you celebrate the memory of your pet.

The Resulting Rewards

The thing that I absolutely love about planning and officiating a pet's funeral or memorial service is that I get to witness the unwavering amount of love and healing that takes place.

Even though there is much sadness, there are moments of incredibly rich emotional sharing with the celebration of a dog's life. I witness life-changing events that people undergo by sharing their life with their cherished dog. I feel honored to be part of those tender moments shared by those who miss their dog and are mourning the loss of their treasured family member.

These are some of those life-changing moments that a pet funeral or memorial service can provide to support the griever in their journey of healing pet loss grief. A pet funeral, pet memorial, or pet remembrance can provide:

- a sense of reality that your pet has reached the end of their life;

- the opportunity for friends and family members to share their thoughts, experiences, and feelings;

- the space for you and others to acknowledge, reflect, and honor the incredible role that the animal played in your lives; and/or

- a healthy way to say a formal good-bye.

A *pet funeral* is generally held within a few days of death and may consist of a viewing, a formal service, and a brief rite at the gravesite. The atmosphere is usually somber and sad, and the emphasis is on death, mourning, and loss.

The funeral can be held at a pet cemetery or in your backyard if your local ordinances allow this. You may invite family, friends, and even other dogs that your dog loved. The ceremony you create can include music, a celebration after the service, and time for others to share their feelings about your dog.

A *memorial service*, on the other hand, may be held at any time after your dog's death. Its function is to remember and celebrate the loved one's life. Oftentimes, the mood is more positive and uplifting. The service can be as small and private, or as open and elaborate, as you wish, and it can be delayed as long as its planning requires. Keep in mind, however, that having the service closer to the time when your loss is most deeply felt is when it is most likely to help you and your family express and work through grief.

Many of my clients who have chosen cremation choose a memorial service that includes spreading the ashes at a favorite locale that their dog loved. Many times a eulogy is also included, a celebration with food afterwards, or even a grand event, such as a hike to a mountain top where the dog loved to go.

Just like a funeral, your memorial service will reflect your unique relationship and will include those things that are meaningful for you.

Pet remembrances are lifelong celebrations. Every year, you can celebrate your dog's birthday by lighting a candle and having a small ceremony. You can also go to your dog's gravesite and leave a favorite toy. You may even want to go to a special place that you and your dog loved and spend a few moments of silence to remember their presence.

Every year for each of my dogs' birthdays, I go to a special place in nature that we enjoyed and read to them a new love letter (chapter 13) that expresses my love for them.

Important Points for Planning

Here are some points you may wish to consider as you plan your own unique ceremony of remembrance for your pet:

- Take some time to plan what you'd like to do. Involve all family members (including children) and others who may be willing to help you.

- Consider whether you want to hold a funeral, a memorial service, or both.

- Given your religious beliefs, traditions, and rituals, determine whether you want to include any religious aspects, or whether you consider their inclusion inappropriate.

- Think of ways the service can be personalized. Ask family members and friends who knew your pet to reminisce with you and recall what was special about your pet.

- Decide who will hold the service, where, when it will be held, who will speak, and who will be invited to attend.

- If you're working with a representative of a pet cemetery or crematory, ask if you can view your pet beforehand and hold the service then.

- Find out what other grieving pet owners have done to honor their pets' memories. Think of ways you can adapt their ideas to make them your own.

- Know that it is both normal and healthy to use a funeral or memorial service to express your sorrow, proclaim your love, and bid a final farewell to your cherished friend.

Chapter Wrap-Up

In this chapter, we covered why it is important to celebrate your dog's life with a pet funeral, memorial, and/or remembrance. You learned the difference between the three and heard the story of Jeremy and Annie and how much having a pet funeral helped them with their journey. Plus, I supplied you with some important points for planning end-of-life ceremonies.

With the chapter's *Contemplation Questions*, you will be able to begin to create your own pet funeral, memorial, and/or remembrance that is special to you and reflects the life that you shared with your dog.

In the next chapter, you are going to learn of a beautiful and extremely healing exercise—writing a love letter to your dog—that can help you keep your dog in your heart and soul.

Chapter 12 Contemplation Questions

How would you like to celebrate your dog's life—a funeral, memorial, and/or remembrance?

Would you include other people, other dogs, and/or other animals? If so, make a list of whom you would invite. Consider if you will ask anyone to speak.

Are you going to write your own eulogy? If so, what will you include?

13. Writing a Love Letter

One of the most important exercises that I share with my clients who are experiencing deep pain and heartache after their dog has died is writing a love letter to their dog to express how much they love them.

A love letter provides a very special way of healing your grief. It is a different way to tell your dog how much you love them. It is a way to express your memories, experiences, and gratitude for the things that you shared with your special pal.

Your mind clutter may be a little chaotic with all your thoughts and feelings at this point. Remember—that is okay. It doesn't matter where you are in your grief journey because writing a love letter to your dog at any time is a wonderful way to heal your pet grief.

No matter where you are with your unique feelings of pet grief, having one place where you can collect and express the love that you have for your dog is extremely helpful. When you can bring together and express your special love bond that you had with your dog in a love letter, it is extremely healing. In writing this letter, you can deepen the connection you had with your furry companion and make a statement of your incredible bond.

Are you not sure where to begin? Are you not really clear how to go about this love letter? That is okay because I am going to help you. I encourage you to spend some time every day jotting down special memories or things that you want to tell your dog—even if it is only five to ten minutes a day that you spend writing down your special memories. Doing so will lead to your writing a personal love letter to your dog.

This letter will be an accumulation of love and thanks from you to your beloved companion. It is your proclamation of appreciation, healing, apology (if needed), and inclusion of anything else that you may want to express to your dog now that they are no longer physically in your life. It is your way to say good-bye in a meaningful way.

My clients who work with me in my *Rescue Joy from Pet Loss Grief* program have found healing and solace when they write love letters. In my course my clients write a series of letters that help them cope with pet loss with grace, respect, and compassion for themselves.

You may be asking, "Why write things down? Why write a love letter? How is that going to help me?" These are common questions and oftentimes writing is not one of the most favorite activities for my clients—until they write the first letter and discover how healing it can be.

Case Study — Karen and Freddy

Karen discovered the positive, restorative rewards when she wrote a love letter to her dog Freddy. Karen discovered that her grief wasn't getting a chance to rule her life once she was actively writing down her thoughts and expressing herself. It was her way to mourn the deep pain that she felt.

At first, Karen wasn't excited about this exercise because she didn't like to write. Then, a beautiful change happened as she began writing down all the lovely memories. Karen discovered that she had forgotten some experiences that she'd had with Freddy, and by writing, she recalled and recaptured the amazing life she'd had with him.

After a few days of collecting all her thoughts, she wrote her first love letter to Freddy. After she read it out loud at Freddy's gravesite, Karen told me, "Writing and reading my love letter to Freddy increased my understanding of how Freddy helped me be a better person. Not only did writing and reading help me express my grief; it helped me realize how much we meant to each other. It made me so happy to celebrate our life together in this way. I can't thank you enough for this exercise. I feel like I had a chance to say good-bye to him."

As her words demonstrate, Karen experienced this exercise as a powerful and healing declaration of her growth and a processing of her grief in a healthy way. Writing a love letter and then reading it out loud helped her with any lingering feelings of pet grief, such as guilt, denial, and anxiety. Plus, it gave her an overwhelming feeling that she was demonstrating a deep and profound respect for Freddy.

Questions to Help Frame Your Love Letter

Each week, I give my clients ten to twelve questions that encourage and support them in choosing a unique way to celebrate the life of their dog for coping and healing. These questions will support you by helping you to determine the feelings of compassion and love that you have for your dog.

Before you answer these questions, have a designated place where you will write your answers. It may be a special journal, your computer, or just a piece of paper. Whatever you choose, be sure to keep all of your answers in one place so that when you are ready to write your love letter, you have everything in front of you.

1. Describe your experience when you first brought your dog home. What happened? How did you feel?

2. Make a list of everything that you and your dog did together. What was the weather like? Where were you? How old were you and your dog? What exactly were you doing? Are there some things that you forgot and remembered again?

3. What was the biggest gift that your dog gave you?

4. Do you have any feelings of guilt or being sorry for something you did or didn't do for your dog? How would you apologize to them beyond just saying, "I am sorry . . . ?"

There is no need to answer these questions all at once unless you are really motivated to do so. In fact, each one of these questions can be dedicated to a single love letter.

When you answer these questions, keep in mind that no one else is going to read them. Write down whatever comes to your mind without judgment and editing. The vital part of this exercise is to get your feelings out on paper so that you are ready to write your love letter with ease.

After you answer all the questions above and maybe some of your own, let your journal sit for a couple of days. You may find you forgot something and want to add it. A memory of you and your dog going for a ride, climbing a mountain, or sleeping all cuddled up in bed might come back to you.

Keep in mind that this letter doesn't have to be perfect. You can write as many letters as you want. Your dog doesn't mind that you spelled something wrong or that your sentence isn't complete.

The more that you can give back to them, the better you are going to feel. Keep in mind this mourning exercise is not time sensitive. If you just lost your dog or it has been months or even years, writing a love letter to them at any time is extremely helpful with processing your grief. I still write letters to all of my dogs, and with each one, I learn something new about our relationship and myself.

Time to Write

After you think you have everything down that you want to tell your dog, it is now time to take out a fresh piece of paper or open a new word document and write your love letter.

The first thing to do is put the date on the top of your letter. The reason for this is that sometime in the future, whether it is months or years from now, you will probably come across the letter. The date will help you put in perspective where you were, and where you now are, in coping with your pet loss grief.

Then start your letter with "Dear [Name of your dog]." I recommend beginning the letter with your dog's given name rather than a nickname because using their given name allows you to have a conversation that is equal and respectful. Also, you can always include any nicknames in the body of the letter.

Next, you start telling your dog all those things that you brainstormed and recorded in response to the questions. If you find that it is difficult to write just one letter, do as many as you want.

The time that you spend on your letter is up to you. Some of my clients spend a little time writing each day for a few days, and some will write their entire letters in one sitting. No matter how you go about it, get the letter done. You will be so happy that you did.

After your letter is written, go to a special place where you are comfortable. It might be a special place that you and your furry friend shared together in nature. It might be at the pet cemetery where your dog is buried (chapter 8), or it may be lying in bed with your dog's favorite toy beside you.

I suggest you do this alone so that you can give your grief and your letter full attention without worrying what someone else thinks of you, your letter, or the fact that you are reading it aloud.

It doesn't matter what others think of your pet grief journey. If you cry, just remember you are experiencing some tough grief here. This entire book is dedicated to supporting you so that you don't feel weird, crazy, or isolated because you are grieving the loss of your dog.

Chapter Wrap-Up

In this chapter we talked about how your relationship with your dog is unique. Your dog loves you, and you love your dog. Cherish that, write them a love letter, go to a special spot when you read it aloud, and feel good about how you are walking this journey of pet loss grief.

The *Contemplation Questions* will continue to guide you through the process of writing and reading your love letter to your dog.

In chapter 14, I am going to continue to support you with your pet grief by including information on what you can expect in your life after your dog has died. We will explore how you can plan for ways in which your life will be different and how you can cope with this.

Chapter 13 Contemplation Questions

In what ways do you think that writing a letter to your dog will help you heal your grief?

How do you feel happy and joyful when you write down the memories that you shared with your companion?

Now that you have written and read your letter to your dog, have any of your feelings of grief lessened or changed? Write that down, so you can reflect on those changes and feel good about them.

14. Anticipating Your New Normal

In this chapter, I am going to continue to support you during another perplexing and possibly challenging time of adjustment for you—your "new normal."

What is your "new normal?" It basically means who you are without your dog—your thoughts, decisions, and changes in outlook in regards to your life.

We will explore what you can expect after your dog has reached the end of their life and they are no longer physically with you. I will share some examples of how your life will change after your dog dies and how you can cope with these changes.

My goal is to continue to help you through this difficult time. I want to give you as many tools as I can so that you feel supported throughout your journey and know what to expect.

Let's begin with a case study in which we learn about Molly's transition to her "new normal" after her loss of Sassafras.

Case Study — Molly and Sassafras

Molly had a very difficult time with the death of Sassafras. They'd done everything together. Every morning they took walks together to visit their neighborhood friends. Sassafras accompanied Molly when Molly ran errands around town.

Sassafras and Molly volunteered at their local library where Molly read stories to the children. Plus, Sassafras was Molly's therapy dog. She helped Molly with regulating her stress and anxiety.

Molly shared with me, "Without Sassafras in my life, I just cannot give myself permission to feel anything other than complete sadness. If I feel happy or joy in my heart, I feel like this would disrespect the bond I shared with her. I am getting tired of people around me telling me that I have been sad long enough or I can get another therapy dog."

Here is the thing about what Molly was experiencing—everything that she said is considered normal grief. She experienced a very huge loss in her life. In expressing what she felt was challenging and important in her life without Sassafras, Molly was beginning to discover her "new normal."

When Molly was ready, I shared with her the following five steps to help her feel supported with discovering her "new normal." Hopefully they will help you as well with what you are experiencing.

Five Steps to a New Normal

1. *A New Identity*

After your dog has died, your life and daily routines are going to change. You are not the same person that shared a life with your beloved companion. The normal activities that you had with your dog are gone, and you will have time that you don't know what to do with.

You no longer have a physical relationship with your dog, and there is a possibility that you will have different beliefs and thoughts as a result of your life with your dog.

Your self-identity will naturally change after your dog dies. This was a change that Molly experienced. She noticed people saying to her, "I remember you—you are the wonderful woman that brought her dog and read to the children. My child loved you and Sassafras."

This is part of your grief journey and something to keep in mind as your life moves forward without your pal.

2. *A New Relationship with Your Dog That Died*

Many of my clients in my Rescue Joy from Pet Loss Grief program work on a common goal—to not forget their dog but to change the relationship from a physical presence to one of wonderful memories or to a spiritual relationship.

There are many ways to do this, and the love letter that you wrote in chapter 13 will help you gain a profound connection by thanking your dog for all the wonderful things that they gave you.

By forming your new identity without your dog and allowing yourself to enjoy memories, you will begin to have a new relationship based on a different type of connection.

In chapter 15, we are going to talk about the afterlife. If you believe in energy connections, I will help you explore ways in which you can connect with your dog on a telepathic level.

3. *A New Group of Friends*

Even though we live in a society that loves its pets, there are some people that don't understand or respect the fact that losing a dog is extremely painful. You may find that after your dog dies, your old friends no longer support you because they become impatient with your grief process. Finding new friends that are more supportive of you is extremely important. For example, you may find yourself relying on and investing more time in relationships with people that are most supportive and not with those that are judgmental.

Also, if you were involved with any dog groups or obedience classes, you developed friendships that included dogs. Not having a dog might create changes in those relationships. You may feel left out or have the feeling they are "too happy."

4. *A New Sense of Purpose*

A common feeling that my clients go through is that they question their purpose in life. Molly did when Sassafras died. She actually thought about giving up the reading program because she felt like Sassafras was a vital part of how she helped the children feel comfortable. She didn't think she could do it alone. She wondered if it was even something purposeful for her anymore.

Like Molly, your dog made a difference in your life, and you depended on each other for happiness and companionship. Now that your dog has died, you may be questioning the meaning of your current existence. This is common and understandable.

Some people realize new life purposes and make significant life changes after their dogs have died. For example, some decide to volunteer at local humane societies, start dog rescue groups of their own, or, like Molly, spend time learning about how their deceased dog can still be part of their life by learning animal communication.

5. *Celebration of Your Growth*

As you experience life without your beloved companion and explore the ways in which your life is changing, your outcome will depend on how you view your new situation.

You didn't choose to experience the loss of your dog. Grief is usually unwanted or unplanned. However, the journey of grief can also be a wonderful experience for personal growth. This type of mourning can be the exact remedy for you to heal your pain.

When you celebrate how you have grown from having shared your heart and soul with your companion, it can help you realize the beautiful and rich life that you had with your dog. It can also help you learn how comfortable you can feel with your new normal.

Some of my clients have learned how to be more sensitive to others by living through their own pain from the losses of their dogs. Others decide to share their hearts and give back to dogs in need. Some learn to celebrate the gifts that their dogs gave them and live their lives in completely different ways.

After Molly worked through these five steps and discovered a different way of dealing with her grief, she was then able to move forward with a different sense of how her life had changed. She eventually began to feel more confident with her unexpected feelings of joy and happiness.

Did Molly's grief go completely away? No, it did not, but it changed and wasn't as raw.

Molly shared with me at the end of the Rescue Joy from Pet Loss Grief program, "I never thought I would be able to survive after Sassafras died. She was my everything. She was my anchor, my purpose, my joy and happiness. When she died, I felt like I didn't deserve to feel these things anymore. But by exploring these five steps on my own time, I was able to realize that what I was feeling was normal and my life was going to be okay."

Molly's experience helped her understand how important it was to know what to expect. It helped her remember that her grief journey was unique to her and normal. With this knowledge she was able to proceed as she wished with her grief journey.

Unexpected, Powerful Experiences

Here are some unexpected things that Molly experienced that you may or may not experience after your dog dies.

You may become aware of:

- some different and unexpected changes in your life;

- a time when you really feel the full extent of your loss;

- ways to redefine your relationship with your deceased dog;

- new discoveries of some areas of personal growth through your pet grief; and/or

- the joy you feel when recalling the memories that you shared together with your four-legged pal.

Remember, this can be a very challenging time period for you. The extent of your loss is felt, and new feelings of grief will emerge.

The Emergence of Your New Normal

During this stretch of time, you will begin to recognize how your life is taking on something we can call your "new normal"—the new thoughts, decisions, and changes in your outlook in regards to your life without your dog.

You may move into a phase of discovering your new normal by taking steps that move you towards understanding life without the physical presence of your dog.

You may spend time with new friends, have different adventures, or do things you have always wanted to do but never did.

You may begin to think about getting another dog or volunteering at your local humane society.

You may even have some feelings of relief, which is common to feel and part of the seven stages of grief that you learned about in chapter 2. If your dog was very ill and suffered a lot during the end of their life, you may feel relieved that they died and are no longer suffering. This too is a feeling that most people experience.

If your dog died suddenly or unexpectedly, this could present you with an entirely different experience and process. Be patient as this type of trauma takes time to process, and you may not be ready to discover your new normal yet.

Remember, there are many things that will happen during this stage of pet loss and grief. They will be unique to you, depending on your experience.

Like grief in general, there will be no prescribed timeframe when you experience these feelings or even have these feelings at all. The relationship that you had with your dog is special to the both of you, and that will never change.

Your dog will live in your heart forever. This is a beautiful blessing that is private and special to the both of you. This place in your heart and the lessons that your dog gave your soul will all influence how you choose to live with the changes in your life.

Your memories of running on the beach, cuddling on the couch, and sharing love will never go away. These pictures are part of you now, living and breathing as you do, and contributing to how you look at life and death. How your grief plays out is the perfect remedy to make choices to change your life.

Let me pause a moment to remind you that this doesn't mean that your active grief will change quickly over the days, weeks, months, and years after your dog dies. It doesn't mean that a new normal will begin to develop right away. It can and probably will take its time.

Another feeling that you may begin to recognize is more joy in your life. Please rest assured, it doesn't mean that you will no longer experience grief from the loss of your dog. It just means that you will begin to feel a shift in your awareness in regards to your grief.

When experiencing your new normal, you will be able to continue to acknowledge and honor your grief, which certainly will resurface. This is what grief is about—it has a life of its own. Yet, during this stage, you will be able to recognize and celebrate your growth and gains as well!

No matter what your experience is during this time, continue to believe in your own process and grow with compassion. Your grief is distinctively yours! It will continue to change so reflect upon what you are going through.

Chapter Wrap-Up

Your new normal is part of the grieving process. By making some changes and experiencing a different type of relationship with your dog, it will never take away the forever bond that you shared with your dog when they were alive.

Please revisit the five steps for discovering your new normal to assist you in dealing with the fact that your dog is no longer physically with you. Each time you review the steps, you will learn, process, and understand something new that can be implemented into your daily journey. Know that you will feel out of place at times, confused, and frustrated—and that is okay.

Your journey with pet grief is unique to you and your dog. Honor your journey with respect and dignity for yourself and your furry companion. No one can alter that if you are aware and accountable for your process.

Use the chapter's *Contemplation Questions* to help you be prepared for your new normal and the action that you can take to heal your pet grief.

If you believe in energy connections and the afterlife, in chapter 15 I share that you can have a forever bond with your dog. If you believe in the spiritual nature of the universe and that energy is infinite, you will get relief in knowing that even though your dog is not with you physically, they are with you in a nonphysical or spiritual existence.

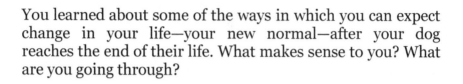

Chapter 14 Contemplation Questions

You learned about some of the ways in which you can expect change in your life—your new normal—after your dog reaches the end of their life. What makes sense to you? What are you going through?

Do you have any feelings of joy or happiness due to what you learned from your dog? Do you feel okay with those feelings?

What are the ways in which you can be sure you receive the support you need when experiencing your "new normal"?

15. Exploring the Afterlife

You have been learning a lot about your grief, how to say good-bye, and ways to deal with the trauma of losing your dog. Most of this information has been very practical. By capturing your heartfelt affection and your love for the special moments that your relationship with your dog gave you, you will find peace with the feelings, emotions, decisions, and options for healing the trauma of losing your dog.

Another important part of your journey is to consider the spiritual aspect of your relationship with your dog. This subject is huge and will be a book of its own in the near future, but for now, I would like to get you started with understanding some of the things that happen to your dog in the nonphysical world.

An important element to understanding the nonphysical world happens via animal mediumship. What animal or pet mediumship refers to is a person experiencing contact with the energy or spirit of their deceased pet through the guidance and expertise of a medium. The role of a medium is to translate and communication messages from a pet that has died to the person that shared their life with the pet. Mediums translate messages from the spiritual to the physical realm by hearing, tasting, sensing, feeling, and seeing.

Although a session with an animal medium is not a cure for the grief that you are going through, it can help ease your pain and misery. Receiving information and messages from your dog in the spiritual realm can assure you that life is eternal.

In my own work as a medium connecting pet owners to their deceased pets, so many people described it as a helpful and reassuring experience. Here is an example of how animal mediumship helped Deb and her dog Lucy.

Case Study — Deb and Lucy

Deb contacted me after the devastating loss of her beloved dog Lucy. She was searching for some answers and trying to make sense of the unexpected loss. Deb, who was in need of support and understanding, found me to be extremely compassionate. I helped her through some difficult days.

What happened was that I used my animal mediumship skills to establish a communication link with Lucy. Through me, Deb got the opportunity to convey her concerns to Lucy and listen to Lucy's messages back to her. It was an amazing experience helping Deb feel a connection with Lucy. Deb told me that it gave her great solace and the much-needed help she'd been searching for.

It had been a lonely time for Deb to be without a dog. So many of her routines were gone, and life was empty. Although Deb tried to stay active with her friends and their dogs, she was experiencing a terrible void.

When Deb was ready to start searching for another dog, a shelter dog came to her attention. After some soul searching, Deb decided that the shelter dog was right for her. As Deb explained it, "I think [the shelter dog] rescued me, rather than me rescuing her. I know that Lucy approves of our choice because of my animal medium session. Also, this new dog has the same swirl fur pattern on her lower back that I thought was unique to Lucy."

Like for Deb, having this communication through a medium can also help to mend your pain of loss, so you can process your grief. By understanding the concept of life after death, you can open your heart to a new relationship with your dog that will never end.

By accepting the fact that energy lives forever, you receive much solace. You will know that your relationship with your dog will continue to deepen and grow, just in a different way.

A Perspective on Death

One way to consider death is to explore the notion that it is a pause between living in physical and nonphysical forms. Your dog will continue loving you and being loyal even after they continue to the afterlife in spirit form. This relationship goes beyond obligation.

You may not feel that you are sensitive enough to be aware of your dog's presence right after death, but your dog may make its presence known to you in a quiet and reassuring way.

They can do this by giving you:

- a brief sighting of them out of the corner of your eye or in a cloud formation;
- a glimpse into their life by way of a dream;
- an opportunity to hear them bark; and/or
- a feeling in your heart that they are close to you.

Case Study — Angie and Racer

My client Angie had a beloved dog named Racer that died of cancer. Angie told me, "My dog Racer died in his sleep in May from terminal cancer. I continued to hear his familiar sounds in the house for ten days after his death. I heard his tail thumping the floor by my bed, his nails tapping on the floor when I came home, and I could even hear him sigh as he did every night before he went to sleep. The sounds always came from where his bed had been."

At first, Angie was a little confused yet happy that she was having these experiences. Once she understood that Racer wanted to make sure she was okay and remind her of his loyalty, she allowed herself to explore the possibility of being receptive to future messages.

Years later, she emailed me and shared, "Every time I am stressed about making a huge decision in my life, Racer comes into my dreams and cuddles up to me. I get the sense he is telling me that I am doing okay. This makes me feel so much better."

When Angie first started to work with me, she had many questions about the afterlife. She feared that Racer was disappearing into nothingness. When she understood that death is the juncture between two worlds, her grief was able to evaporate some.

This is not to say you won't feel suddenly desperate or alone when the death of your dog has occurred. The silence and stillness of their body can be a traumatic experience and bring up many unexpected emotions. Yet, when you can witness through an energy connection that your dog's body is physically free of pain and suffering, it can help you gain solace by knowing that when they are in spirit, they do not feel pain.

Even knowing this, there are many questions that you may have. I am going to share with you five of the most common questions that I receive from my clients.

Common Questions Concerning the Afterlife

Question #1 – What happens when my dog dies?

When your furry companion dies, they move into spiritual energy or existing as a soul spirit. They exist without sickness, pain, or fear. Your dog in energy form is cherished and respected for the work they did with you on Earth, which is extremely honorable. Since they are living in spirit, their role is to prepare and transition for their next role.

Right after they die, there is a transition period that can take up to two weeks. This may be the time that you see, feel, hear, and/or sense their presence. Know that it is okay. They are just making the transition in their own way and reminding you they love you.

Question #2 – Why did my dog behave the way they did before dying?

If your dog exhibited any new behaviors days, hours, or minutes before dying, this was their way of transitioning their energy. There will be a period of time when they are in-between bodies, which means they are partly in the physical form yet they haven't quite made the full transition into death or the spiritual form.

Question #3 – Does my dog that died have a special message for me?

The answer is YES! When a dog dies, they are still contactable and often want to continue to contact their people for many years. Even though they are not in the physical body, their spirit is alive and well. You can still see, hear, or sense your dog, even if for a fleeting moment.

When they do contact you, there is purpose in that connection, so having an animal medium help you sort out this message can be helpful. You can consider your dog as your lifetime guide or guru, helping you to find peace amongst the chaos of being human.

Question #4 – Will my animal come back to live with me?

They can and they do! They will come back as an animal companion. Animals do not reincarnate as humans.

Also, parts of their "personality" can also come back as part of another pet's personality.

My dog Addie definitely is part-Marley and part-Kado! She has some of the same endearing antics that only Kado had and shows Marley's energy of healing. Addie has her own spiritual traits as well. She is still a puppy, so she is evolving, but one of her spiritual traits is the ability to move through new experiences without letting fear take over.

Question #5 – Does my dog know that they are going to die?

Yes, they do! Dogs are fine-tuned and highly evolved beings. They are part of the divine plan to help us be better human beings. They are okay with death, so when they die, it means that their work with us is complete, according to their Earth plan, and that they taught us what we needed to know.

Even though your dog knew they were going to die and entered into a new soul-spirit life, they are always accessible to you. By quieting your soul or spirit, you will be able to contact them and hear what they have to say. My clients are often calmed and relieved when they get their special messages from their dear animal friends.

Chapter Wrap-Up

Connecting with your dog in the afterlife is a healthy way to cope with your grief. Listening to what your dog has to say in spirit form will increase your forever bond in a new way.

If you are having a difficult time with the fact that your dog is no longer physically with you, please revisit the five steps to discovering your "new normal" in chapter 14 and consider doing an animal mediumship session to get some answers to your questions. This will help you feel comfortable with this stage of healing.

Your journey with the loss of your dog is unique to you and your dog. Although your dog is now in spirit form, they are still reachable. You can do this on your own or with the help of an animal medium.

Here are your final *Contemplation Questions* to help you explore the option of connecting with your dog in the afterlife. Dedicate yourself to these questions only if you believe in this concept or only when you are ready.

Chapter 15 Contemplation Questions

What are your experiences of "sensing" your dog's presence?

Have you had any dreams of your dog? What do you think is the message your dog wants to share with you through the dream?

How are you still spiritually connected to your dog?

Final Thoughts

You and your dog shared an incredible life together. These times were special occasions for you that you will always cherish and hold in your heart. You experienced many escapades, joys, and adventures that will continue to help you understand all that life with a dog has to offer.

Together you gave each other an incredible sense of belonging, purpose, and joy. Your dog connected you to other animals, people, nature, the universe, and new ways of looking at life. Their ability to listen, teach, and heal was acquired when you listened to them and acted upon the lessons they showed and shared with you.

Your dog gave you stability when you couldn't get that from family, friends, and coworkers. Together you made each other's life full of purpose, a little easier, and much more fun.

Learning about living life in the present and freeing the soul to experience happiness is what your dog exceled in. They never wavered from this. Your dog constantly reminded you to never give up on yourself and that you are awesome. Your dog taught you to spend your valuable time with people and adventures that matter most.

The daily conversations that you had with your dog were profound, life-changing, and sometimes silly. Your dog had the uncanny ability to help you see things for what they truly were. Your dog changed your outlook on life.

Without judgment, complaint, or impatience, your dog listened to your secrets that many a human being would never consider doing or will never know about you. The confidentiality that you shared with your dog was your special pact, a special bond not to be accessed by any other living being.

It is, therefore, your right to feel raw, angry, sad, depressed, etc., now that your dog has died and they are no longer snuggled by your side. This unavoidable event that ultimately happens in every dog lover's life is mind-crushing and heart-splitting. And some just don't understand. When your dog is ripped from your life, you can expect changes and some not all that comfortable.

You can expect that you are going to feel chaotic, isolated, irritated, ravenous, perplexed, bewildered, mixed-up, and all the other normal and common feelings of grief.

In order to soothe your soul, keep in mind that your bond with your dog was not shared by anyone else. It was entirely exclusive and exceptional to the both of you. Therefore, what you experience is going to reflect your personality, your dog's personality, and all the things that you shared together.

Your job now is to mourn and experience the changes in your life without your pup. Learn from them and ultimately fill your heart again with the joy that is now lost.

You are going to experience that some people are just not going to get what you are going through and will encourage you to move on before you are ready. That is okay. It is not your job to change their opinions. Turn your attention to your memories and your dog.

Be ready for the fact that you will be faced with some tough and annoying decisions that will demand your attention, and that is what you can spend your valuable energy on to fully process your loss. You want to be able to make these decisions without regret, guilt, or remorse.

The important thing to do is to get in touch with your feelings of grief and learn how they are going to help you throughout your life. Do not allow the non-believers to take your beautiful memories from your heart.

Mourn your emotions and celebrate the life of your dog with supportive and non-judgmental friends, family, support groups, or a pet loss coach. Through this experience, you are going to find a remedy for your personal pain by taking care of yourself, your beliefs, and the gifts that you received from your dog.

Your life purpose and journey will not end now that your dog has died. Instead, you will gain some incredible insight that will split your heart open to receive a continued relationship with them on a spiritual level if you so choose. Your life will be enriched and soulfully balanced.

The changes you are experiencing and your feelings of being abandoned by your companion result in a tremendous impact in the way you are now moving through life. This book took you by the hand and supported you with tools and options on how you can walk this part of your pet loss voyage with a warm heart and a gentle nudge. I hope you took me up on my offer of the free, downloadable guided Healing Dog Loss Meditation mp3. By engaging in this short meditation, daily or even a few times a week, you will only soften the rough patches of your journey of grief.

With my program Rescue Joy from Pet Loss Grief, which is your next step after this book, you can continue to receive support as you continue the journey. This time-tested program that has already helped many others has been created with you in mind to bring you wisdom and personal growth, so you can reach a place of profound understanding that is different from what you are experiencing now. If you would like to experience support on this level, please go to the resources section to contact me.

Jan, who lost her beloved Wally, explained the *Rescue Joy from Pet Loss Grief* program in this way:

> *"Without this program, I don't think I would have been able to get through the tough days. What it did for me was give me hope, perspective, and inspiration to continue. I was able to focus on my grief, mourn, and create a deep respect for the life that I shared with Wally. Without this course, I would have been focusing on all the stuff that would keep me believing all the myths that society expects us to believe about life, death, and the afterlife. Wendy and her course helped me experience and trust my knowledge, intuition, and process."*

Like Jan, trust that your ultimate journey is a reflection of what you experienced and what you are experiencing now. The life you had while your dog was physically with you will give you the inspiration and accountability to develop a different connection with your dog that will last your lifetime.

When you are ready to celebrate your dog with a pet funeral, memorial, or celebration-of-life ceremony, you will be actively making a commitment to your dog and recognizing them as an integral part of your life, family, and personal growth. Your dog was your best friend, and you are healthy to mourn the loss of them by creating a special service of celebration.

When you enjoy the memories that you shared with your dog, it will help you experience your grief in a healthy way.

Resources

Ways in which I can support you

Center for Pet Loss Grief: Through Life, Death, and Beyond
Wendy Van de Poll, MS, CEOL

https://centerforpetlossgrief.com

Best Selling and Award Winning Books
https://centerforpetlossgrief.com/books

My Dog IS Dying: What Do I Do?
My Dog HAS Died: What Do I Do?

My Cat IS Dying: What Do I Do?
My Cat HAS Died: What Do I Do?

Healing A Child's Pet Loss Grief

Free Book
Healing Your Heart From Pet Loss Grief

Free Pet Grief Support Kit
https://centerforpetlossgrief.com

Animal Mediumship
https://centerforpetlossgrief.com/animal-medium

Animal Communication
https://wendyvandepoll.com/animal-communication

Pet Funerals
https://centerforpetlossgrief.com/pet-funeral

Facebook
Center for Pet Loss Grief
https://facebook.com/centerforpetlossgrief

Pet Memorial Support Group
https://facebook.com/groups/petmemorials.
centerforpetlossgrief

Veterinarians:

Veterinary Medical Association
www.ahvma.org/

Home Euthanasia and Pet Hospice Veterinarians
www.iaahpc.org/

Online Product Support:

Herbal Support: Pet Wellness Blends Affiliate
www.herbs-for-life-3.myshopify.com/#_l_1e

Magnetic Therapy Supplies: aVivoPur Affiliate
www.avivopur.com/#_a_CenterForPetLossGrief

Heart in Diamonds: Affiliate
www.heart-in-diamonds.com/?aff=CenterForPetLoss

Support Groups:

Association for Pet Loss and Bereavement
www.aplb.org/

International Association for Animal Hospice and Palliative Care
www.iaahpc.org/

Association for Human-Animal Bond Veterinarians
www.aahabv.org/

Book 3 in The Pet Bereavement Series

My Cat Is Dying: What Do I Do?

Emotions, Decisions, and Choices for Healing Pet Loss

Thinking about life without your cat isn't something you probably want to do right now. However, you just got the news from your veterinarian that the test results expose the horrible fact—your cat is terminally ill.

Your cat brings so much joy and love to your life that it makes you sick to your stomach to think she is going to die soon. You can't bear the thought, and your mind right now is starting to get muddled with all kinds of thoughts, like:

- *What am I going to do?*

- *How can I get her better?*

- *Why do I feel like I want to get mad at someone?*

Know that you are beginning to experience what is called "normal grief." Even still, you are deeply confused and hurt by what is happening to your cat and you.

As a responsible cat person, you know that illness and death are inevitable for cats just as is true for humans. However, that doesn't lessen the magnitude of your grief and the anxiety over what you are going to do to help your cat be as comfortable as she can.

This book is for you—the cat lover who is faced with the fact that your cat is ill and may not have much longer to live. This book is going to be your new best friend, always there for you with helpful tips, guidance, and options for achieving peace of mind.

If you just got the news that your cat is terminally ill and you are faced with crazy emotions, difficult decisions, and hard choices that you don't want to make, I am going to offer tools to support you through the turmoil of caretaking a terminally ill cat. In this book, I am going to supply you with options, so you can begin to heal your grief as well as spend quality time with your cat during this time.

My Cat Is Dying: What Do I Do? has been written just for you. It is your emotional emergency first-aid kit that will support you during this wild ride that you are about to take and that you weren't planning on taking for a long time.

I know these feelings well as I have been there with many of my clients, supporting them with healing their pet loss.

I GET GRIEF, and in my experience as a pet loss grief coach I have found that . . .

1. As humans, we all experience grief, and we can't avoid it. It is part of life.

2. It is healthy to express our grief rather than stuff it in. Stuffing it in only makes it worse. It can be difficult to express yourself, and it does take work, but in the long run—you will feel better.

3. It is extremely important to find a supportive friend, group, or end-of-life coach that will provide a calm place for you to express your grief. Not many people are comfortable with the grieving process, so choose wisely.

Your grieving process when you learn about your cat's illness is delicate, unique, and important to you. When your furry companion is dying, your life suddenly is not normal anymore. This process can take time.

Book 3: My Cat Is Dying: What Do I Do? will help you create a compassionate, respectful, healthy, and loving journey for you and your cat to share during this tough, yet special, time.

Remember, you are not alone with what you are experiencing, especially with your pet loss grief.

To receive notification when this book is published, please go to www.centerforpetlossgrief.com/free-gift and we'll put you on the mailing list after you download your free gift.

Acknowledgments

First I would love to express my deepest compassion to all of my clients and readers who feel safe with walking the challenging journey of healing pet loss. Trusting and believing that their rawness is okay.

My heart and empathy goes to the stories of Katharine and Dino, Martha and Teddy, Deb and Lucy, Debi and Niko, Anne and Ruby, Carmon and Jetson, Cissy and Crystal, Roberta and Chester Bell, Ellissa and Lester, Piper and Dandelion, Barbara and Noogett, Susanne and Trixi, Pam and Mergie, Tim, Carol, Emily and Max, Robin, Travis and Mecco, Sandy, Ralph and Sophia, Trisha and Boomer, Veronia and Cracker, Jeremy, Annie and Oscar, Karron and Freddy, Molly and Sassafras and Angie and Racer.

I would also like to show my deepest appreciation for my writing coach Ramy Vance and the folks at Self-Publishing School that have guided me to follow my life long passion to become a bestselling author. My SPS family and my Launch Team members are the best!

I am truly in awe of my editor Nancy Pile who once again added her heart and paws to bring my book to another level. Debbie Lum for her beautiful formatting and Danijela Mijailovic for her gorgeous book cover artistry.

To Marley, Kado, Maya and the rest of my fur, feather and fin gurus who continue to hold my heart through vital life lessons that I am determined to accomplish. They are amazing and wise teachers.

My husband Rick is the best. His over-the-moon-support is something this lucky woman gets to experience every single day of her life! Thank you my dear sweet husband, mwah.

About the Author

Wendy Van de Poll is a pioneering leader in the field of pet loss grief support. Wendy is dedicated to providing a safe place for her clients to express their grief over the loss of their pets.

What makes Wendy successful with her clients is that she get's grief! *"Over the years I've dealt with my own grief and helping many families communicate and connect with their pets long after their loss. It's what I've done since I was just 5 yrs old!"*

She is compassionate and supportive to all who know her.

Her passion is to help people when they are grieving over the loss of a pet and her larger than life love for animals has led her to devote her life to the mission of increasing the quality of life between animals and people no matter what stage they are in their cycle of life! She has been called the animal whisperer.

She is a Certified End of Life and Pet Grief Support Coach, Certified Pet Funeral Celebrant, Animal Medium and Communicator and Licensed Massage Therapist for Human, Horse and Hound. She is the founder of The Center for Pet Loss Grief and an international best selling and award-winning author and speaker.

She holds a Master's of Science degree in Wolf Ecology and Behavior and has run with wild wolves in Minnesota, coyotes in Massachusetts and foxes in her backyard. She lives in the woods with her husband, two crazy birds, her rescue dog Addie and all kinds of wildlife.

Wendy currently has a Skype, phone, and in-person practice, providing end-of-life and pet grief support coaching, animal communication, animal mediumship, and personalized pet funerals.

You can reach her at www.centerforpetlossgrief.com/contact

Thank You for Reading

My Dog Has Died: What Do I Do?
Making Decisions and Healing the Trauma of Pet Loss

Hi, my name is Addie or Ms. Addie-Pants, as my mom likes to call me. As you can see I am ready to play and happy that you read this book! Since this book is dedicated to me, it would mean a lot if you left a review on Amazon by visiting this link: www.amzn.com/B01GBQW9W8

I came from Texas on December 9, 2014 to live in New Hampshire. Wendy didn't know it yet but as a 10-week old puppy, found in a box on the side of a busy highway, I had a divine plan for her.

In truth, my mom was feeling sad about Marley who died on September 25, 2014. Her heart was raw and split open. My job was to melt into her heart and heal the pain she was feeling – from the inside out. Well, guess what? As soon as she saw me (first one to hold me) it happened – our hearts melted together and the healing began!

My goal for this book is to help support you along with my mom and show you how to heal your heart – allowing it to mend. With patience, love and respect your journey will be softer. As a rescue dog, I know that really well!

I loved that my mom wrote this book to help you on your grieving journey. I would be grateful if you would leave a helpful review on Amazon:

Please go to this link www.amzn.com/B01GBQW9W8 to leave your review.

Thank you,

Ms. Addie-Pants
The Mensa Puppy

The Pet Bereavement Series
Best Selling and Award Winning Books

By Wendy Van de Poll, MS, CEOL

My Dog IS Dying: What Do I Do?
My Dog HAS Died: What Do I Do?

My Cat IS Dying: What Do I Do?
My Cat HAS Died: What Do I Do?

Healing A Child's Pet Loss Grief

Free Book

Healing Your Heart From Pet Loss Grief

CPSIA information can be obtained
at www.ICGtesting.com
Printed in the USA
BVHW031751290820
587590BV00001B/342

9 780997 375619